This edition published in 2007 by
Carlton Books Limited, 20 Mortimer Street, London W1T 3JW

Copyright © Éditions Prolongations 2007
Translation copyright © Carlton Books Limited 2007

A CIP catalogue record for this book is available from the British Library

ISBN: 978-1-84442-189-3

Project editor: Martin Corteel
Design and layout: Cazarama
Production: Peter Hinton

Unless otherwise stated, all quotations reproduced in this book have been taken from the publications of SNC L'Equipe: *L'Equipe* • *L'Equipe Magazine* • *France Football* • *Foot 2*

Printed in Dubai

Bad boys Of Football

John
Phillips

CARLTON
BOOKS

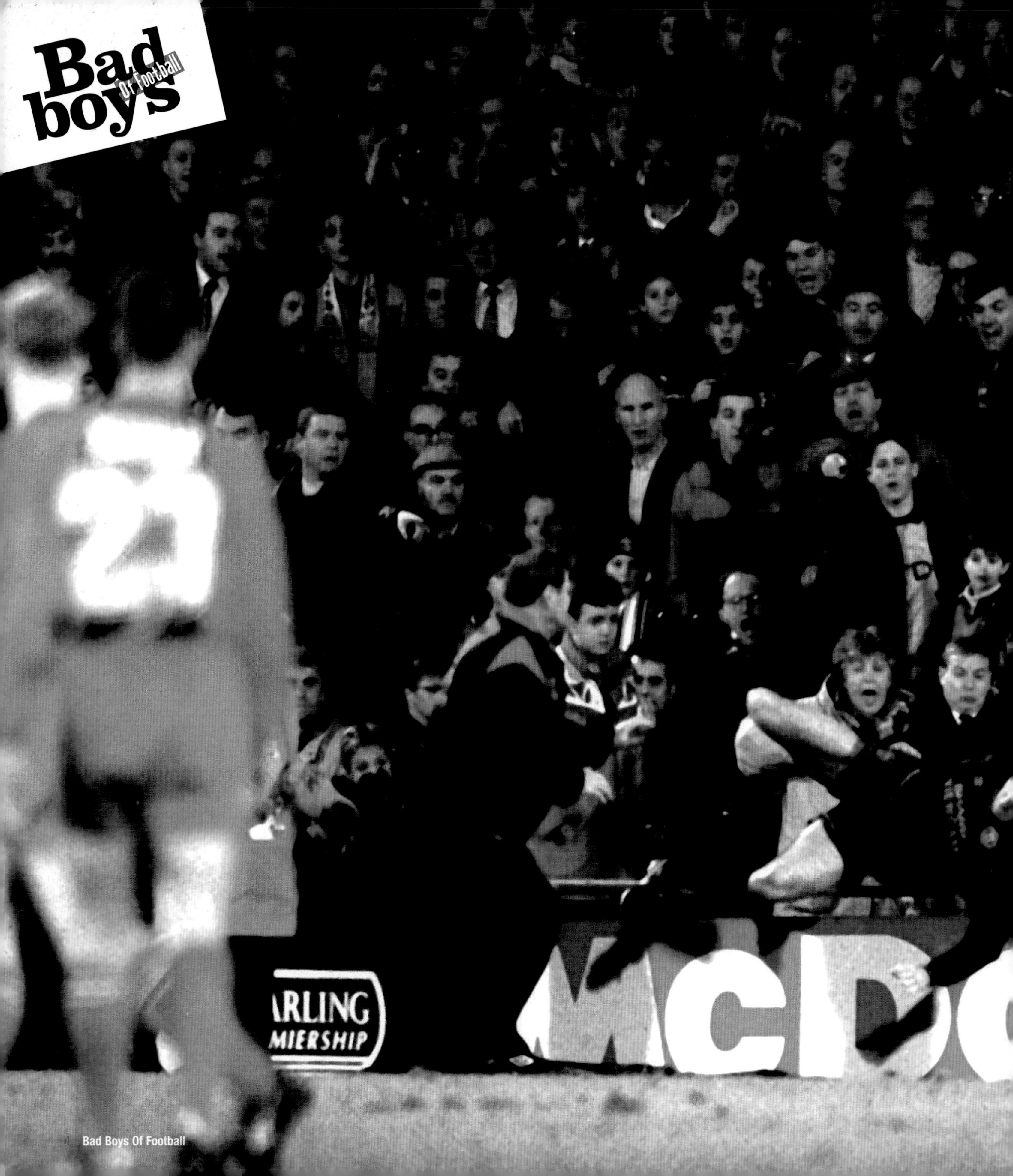
ARLING
MIERSHIP

"In football, there have always been some things that are settled on the pitch."

MARCO MATERAZZI

"You can let the
man or the ball past,
but never both!"

PEDRO MONZON

The «Bad boy» ATTITUDE

There are many footballers who would have liked to be featured in this book, and will be disappointed not to be. There are strict selection criteria to become part of the "bad boys" family. It's not just a matter of losing it once on the pitch through having a rush of blood. You have to show consistency and determination in extreme behaviour, provocation, wild rages, obscenely high tackles, brawls outside nightclubs. You don't need one red card; you need lots. The "bad boy attitude" doesn't just happen. It's a way of life, an enviable status that you don't get just by having one or two punishments dished out.

Bad boys will never be "standard", according to Eric Cantona. They are the *enfants terribles* of football who are undeniably terribly different. They're hard men, wind-up merchants, drinkers, cruisers, boasters, paranoiacs, geniuses; they're rough, unstable, egocentric, eccentric … And they all stand out sharply from the crowd of sensible footballers. They are superior – or at least think they are – sometimes talking about themselves in the third person, and believe, or pretend to, that they are on earth for a special reason. But all bad boys share a common trait, the unwavering certainty, whether rightly or wrongly, that they're not like all the others, and they don't mind letting us know … The bad boy brings it on. Whatever his faults or excesses, there's never an act of contrition, and there's never an excuse for daring to do things that others would not. Maradona, Cantona, Best … they're the inspired masters of football from another planet.

Pampered, idolized, they can do anything they want, right up to the final act of self-destruction. They don't recognize constraints. The only authority they respect is that of raw talent and they refuse to bow to the orders of trainers, coaches or even national team managers. Threats, punishments, fines and suspensions have no effect. On the pitch and off, they follow their instincts. When learning the trade, no one taught them to cross the pitch solo and dribble the ball past one opponent after the other. The bad boy genius does this at the very highest level. "I was born with a talent that some would die for," said George Best once in a thoughtful moment. "I could do things no other footballer could and could do them with ease. I knew I was different and, in the end, I became a monster in my own eyes."

As Argentine anthropologist and writer, Eduardo Archetti, once wrote about Maradona, the talented "El Pibe" (the Kid): "He was born with such a huge talent, no one could ever teach him a thing about his game. He didn't need an authority figure or a mentor. He saw his talent as a victory over discipline and group order."

Becoming heroes of modern times on the back of intense media hype, these Chosen Ones have created vocations for themselves. But not all the wrangling and bad-tempered players you see on the pitch have the talent of a Vinnie Jones or a Gennaro Gattuso, even if some do seem to think that they can find a path to glory by copying the behaviour of the real bad boys.

It may well be that the general fascination with these icons has led some of the less talented, in football terms, to behave like thugs in the hope of finding a place in the sun. In England, Lee Bowyer and Jonathan Woodgate, in the tradition of a Nobby Stiles, the famous butcher of the 1960s, have never balked at leaving behind a few scars, either on the pitch or in nightclubs. They have taken on board the words of Paul Ince, another fan of hacking down the opposition, but who hasn't done enough to carve himself a place in this book: "A really aggressive game based on tackles is what the Manchester United fans want to see. Guys who work hard all week and pay for their seats always like players like me."

You have to remember that even falling into bad boy habits such as talking about yourself in the third person or bursting into tears as soon as emotion kicks in at the end of a match doesn't automatically make you a Stoichkov or a Maradona. To gain access to this envied footballing elite, the prospective bad boy must demonstrate unfailing nerve and tenacity.

Often described as charming, full of kindness and attentive once off the pitch, aren't these bad boys actually just inspired, if awkward, apostles of freedom? Why, when it comes down to it, have we made them part of this rather shameful cult? It's undoubtedly because, apart from their sometimes (self-) destructive excesses, they embody new possibilities in a game that's increasingly formatted. Regardless of whether they are, as we have categorized them, proper one-off champions, proper hard men or proper pains, they are the ones who transgress, breaking the rules of the game and the rules of decorum and, consequently, are the ones who take football to that other dimension that the crowds will always love.

JOHN PHILLIPS

Bad boys Of football

George Best

Paul Breitner

Eric Cantona

Paul Gascoigne

Diego Maradona

Lothar Matthaeus

Hristo Stoichkov

Zinedine Zidane

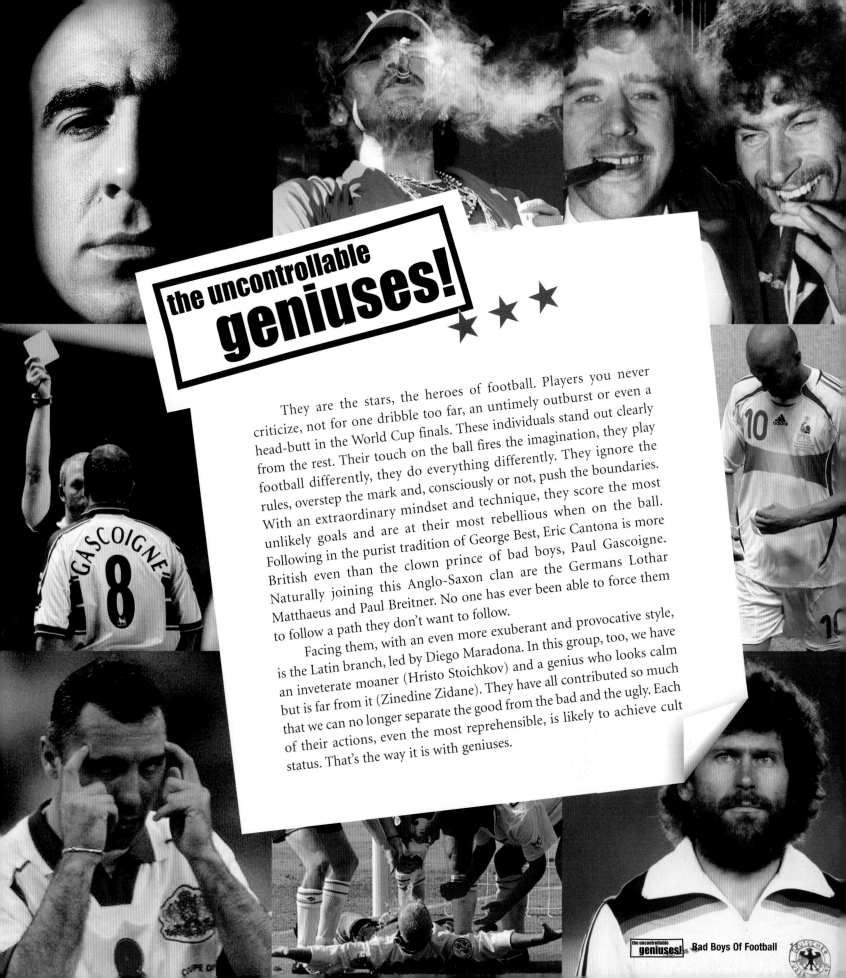

the uncontrollable geniuses!

★ ★ ★

They are the stars, the heroes of football. Players you never criticize, not for one dribble too far, an untimely outburst or even a head-butt in the World Cup finals. These individuals stand out clearly from the rest. Their touch on the ball fires the imagination, they play football differently, they do everything differently. They ignore the rules, overstep the mark and, consciously or not, push the boundaries. With an extraordinary mindset and technique, they score the most unlikely goals and are at their most rebellious when on the ball. Following in the purist tradition of George Best, Eric Cantona is more British even than the clown prince of bad boys, Paul Gascoigne. Naturally joining this Anglo-Saxon clan are the Germans Lothar Matthaeus and Paul Breitner. No one has ever been able to force them to follow a path they don't want to follow.

Facing them, with an even more exuberant and provocative style, is the Latin branch, led by Diego Maradona. In this group, too, we have an inveterate moaner (Hristo Stoichkov) and a genius who looks calm but is far from it (Zinedine Zidane). They have all contributed so much that we can no longer separate the good from the bad and the ugly. Each of their actions, even the most reprehensible, is likely to achieve cult status. That's the way it is with geniuses.

George Best

THE LORD AND MASTER

"I spent most of my money on booze

George Best

and birds. The rest I just squandered."

What do we admire most about George Best? The footballer's style or his flamboyant lifestyle, taking him from the arms of a Miss World to behind the bars of American jails? Well, both, of course. What obviously fascinates us about this man from Northern Ireland is the total freedom with which he lived life on and off the pitch. He was, and was always, a bad boy through and through, their lord and master. "Best literally flew through matches, embodying freedom on the pitch more than anyone else. It was the ease. He was untouchable. He could dribble the ball past three, four or five players. And he was rock and roll." These are the words of Eric Cantona, another inveterate Manchester United bad boy, for whom Best was "the fifth Beatle". Like Best, Cantona wore the No. 7 at Manchester United.

Having the name "Best" isn't easy. Especially when you come from Belfast in Northern Ireland, you're told you're too skinny to play football by local clubs and you debut at Manchester United at the age of 17, under the legendary, shrewd manager Matt Busby, having taken the ferry to accompany a mate wanting to try his luck in the English game of the 1960s.

"I was born with a talent that some would die for. I could do things no other footballer could and could do them with ease. I knew I was different and, in the end, I became a monster in my own eyes." >

"Go for it, go for it from the first minute. This principle should take you through life too."

This is how George Best defined himself in his autobiography, *The Good, the Bad and the Bubbly*, published in 1990. A wicked gift, too much of a good thing, making you feel different and making you wicked. "If football can be considered an art, then I was an artist," Best was to say in his twilight years, analysing his amazing talent for wrong-footing an opponent, which he would strive to squander all through the 1970s in unlikely clubs, notably on the west coast of the United States.

In 1968 Best, who hadn't yet managed to destroy his incredible dribbling skills through his love for J&B, won the European Cup with Man Utd against Benfica Lisbon (4–1 after extra time). He was also crowned top scorer in England with 28 goals and received the France Football Golden Ball award at the end of the season, the most prestigious award for a European footballer.

He was not even 22 years old. He drove a Jaguar and wore fuchsia shirts and flared trousers. He opened fashion boutiques, a travel agency, nightclubs and bars, inevitably. He had a futurist house built in the country outside Manchester. He could do anything he wanted, without sanction. Drunk driving, brazen pulling, brawls … He took advantage ad nauseam. "I've never been faithful to anyone and it's become a sport, a game of numbers, a way of filling the void. I had no restrictions between 1960 and 1970. No one worried about how many times and with how many partners. The numbers only increased: actresses, waitresses, sales assistants, sisters, mother and daughter (at the same time), three-in-a-bed …" His declarations delighted the sensationalist press. "I was acquainted with Miss Canada, then Miss United Kingdom, then Miss World. Ultimately, my life is quite dull."

The legendary dynamism he displayed at Old Trafford, however, appeared in another guise, less popular with the crowd. George Best was arrogant, confrontational, desperate and appalling. He overdid everything, turning his excesses into a trademark. "I've always had this obsession – to do better than everyone else at everything – on the pitch, at the bar, with the birds, with designer clothes … If I had to make a choice between beating four Liverpool defenders and then planting a goal in the top corner or scoring with one of the Miss Worlds, I'd have trouble choosing. Luckily, I had the chance to do both, so I didn't have to."

His rock star lifestyle did not marry well with the demands of a professional footballer. Constantly looking to push the boundaries, Best came up against his first brick wall in January 1970. He was suspended for four weeks for snatching the ball from the hands of a referee. On his return, he scored six goals in an 8–2 FA Cup victory over Northampton, but was sent off again during a Northern Ireland match, this time for throwing mud at the referee. His lateness and mood swings increased to the point that Matt Busby suspended him for two weeks in January 1971. >

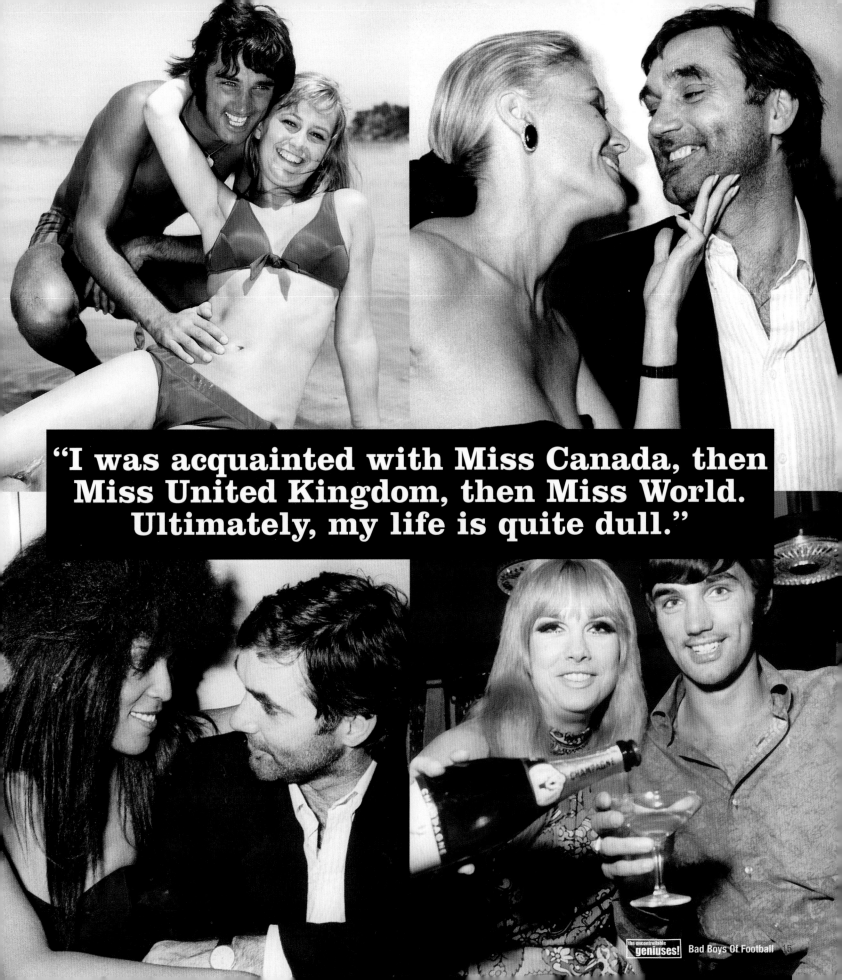

"I was acquainted with Miss Canada, then Miss United Kingdom, then Miss World. Ultimately, my life is quite dull."

The English FA proved stricter, handing out a six-month suspension. But this had no effect. Even confined to living with the Man Utd juniors, with his salary halved, Best continued doing as he pleased. "Since they treated me as irresponsible, I began to behave irresponsibly. I became a rebel."

In May 1972, he left his team and disappeared to Marbella, where the English tabloid paparazzi followed him and snapped him in the company of creatures whose only similarity with a ball, you could say, were their curves. The lack of competitiveness of the Northern Ireland team would continue to hurt him deeply. Because of this, he would never experience the frissons of a world competition. "I'd have been able to put up with anything had I known the success of a Pele or Maradona."

In January 1974, at the age of 28, George Best ended his adventure with Manchester United (466 matches and 178 goals), after being told he was to be on the bench for the Plymouth game. He left the stadium in tears and disappeared. "We play out our talents in a wasteful country," he later commented. Manchester United's manager, Tommy Docherty, ended his contract.

Best then made a series of brief appearances for Irish, Scottish, Australian and, above all, American clubs. In 1976 he signed a two-and-a-half year contract with the Los Angeles Aztecs. He scored goals (15) and drank, stylishly cultivating the art of provocation. "I had a house by the sea. But I had to pass a bar to go to the beach, so I never saw the sea." In 1978 he joined up with former British stars Gordon Banks and Ian Callaghan at Fort Lauderdale, and in 1980 he played for San Jose Earthquakes. After he finished playing, in 1983, he settled in London.

Still well known, he cashed in on his celebrity and his shrewd understanding of the game and became a pundit. On television, he often announced the outcome of a movement before it had happened. But he wasn't always reliable, forgetting appointments or just sleeping through them. The channel kept having to provide a replacement. At the age of 50, he looked like an old man, bloated and ravaged from alcohol. His face wore the "kiss of Belfast", as he himself called it: 268 stitches following countless fights.

"When I walk around London, I always come across someone who wants to fight with me. Kids of 17 or 18, thugs, but I don't give a damn. I can deal with them, they don't often get the upper hand. I like to keep myself to myself and stay out of trouble, but there's always an arsehole looking for me, wanting to prove he's the boss to his mates. This happens every day, every day of my bloody life. I could try to avoid it, go and live alone elsewhere. But that would be admitting that they've won, and I don't like letting them win."

Best's cutting style on the air was popular, and he even gave a choice verdict on the golden boy, the new idol of English football, the antithesis of the bad boy, David Beckham. "He can't kick with his left foot, he can't head a ball, he can't tackle and he doesn't score many goals. Apart from that, he's all right."

Among the famous quotes of "Georgie the lush", this one remains in our memories, conferring on him the definitive title of lord and master of the bad boys: "I spent most of my money on booze and birds. The rest I just squandered." But, perhaps it is his message to footballers that should be remembered: "Go for it, go for it from the first minute. This principle should take you through life too."

After a number of alcohol-induced comas, various detoxification remedies, a lengthy hospital stay in 2001 and then a liver transplant in 2002, George Best died on November 25, 2005 at the age of 59. Several days later, more than three hundred thousand people turned out for his funeral in Belfast. ■

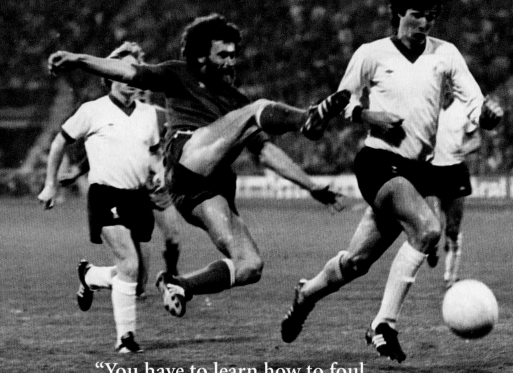

"You have to learn how to foul.
Football is a combat sport, more attacking than judo or karate. Football is like
boxing. Contact is an everyday part of the game."

Paul
Breitner

THE AWFUL AFRO

One of his friends should no doubt have told him that you shouldn't tell the whole truth. That sometimes a little tact and diplomacy is needed, and that even the purists of the game win by toning it down sometimes. The problem is Paul Breitner had few friends and, just as a wine lover wouldn't water down a fine wine, he wouldn't compromise his personality. It was undeniable that the boy with the golden legs was the world's best defender at the beginning of the 1970s, and he was more intelligent than the other players in the Bundesliga.

With his athletic form, standing just short of six feet and weighing less than 11.5 stone, he made his debut at Kolbermoor before joining the amateur team at Frellassing. He finally turned professional at Bayern Munich. In 1970, he played his first league match at 18 years of age and earned immediate respect as a left-back. With his long black beard and unruly hair, he was nicknamed "Der Afro". He laid it on thick, and although evidently a rough player, he never received a single red card, and was a faultless receiver of the ball. He was a key figure in the Bayern of Beckenbauer, Müller, Hoeness, Schwarzenbeck and Maier, and the national team too, since it was made up essentially of Bayern players.

The tough player subjected himself to endurance and body-building sessions that made his team-mates tremble. "I've actually always hated exercising," confessed the man with *that* beard, "but it's essential to progress physically and ensure you're capable of playing at the very highest level."

At the age of 22, he had already won everything a footballer could hope to win over an entire career: the 1972 European Championship, the 1974 World Cup, the 1974 European Cup, the German League (1972, 1973, 1974) and the German Cup (1971).

There's an African proverb – there's only room for one crocodile in a creek – which "the Afro" seems to have made all his own. In the German national team there were several already, and at the outset they happily welcomed the newcomer. Team-mates Franz Beckenbauer and Gerd Muller even taught the young Breitner how to sneak out the night before a match, or how to make a deal with the hotel chef to ensure he saves you the best cut of pork and that you can get a snack at four in the morning. All this was amusing for a while, but the orders of "Kaiser Franz" quickly bored him. He drank

Paul Breitner

beer and posed in lederhosen with the others, but proclaimed his Maoist beliefs. He was photographed under the portrait of Mao Zedong. "I was politically active at the beginning of the 1970s," laconically commented the man for whom the United States was the best country in the world.

Moaning, unsatisfied and demanding, he openly criticized his team-mates, despite his team's success. The atmosphere was so bad within the national team that he threatened to leave the group several hours before the start of the 1974 World Cup. "Muller and I had to stay up all night talking to Paul to persuade him to stay," remembers Franz Beckenbauer. "The argument that swung it was that at this time of night and out in the sticks, where our hotel was, he would never find a car to take him to the station. What was he going to do, hitch?"

Breitner stayed and, without him, Germany would never have won the World Cup, although their victory is generally attributed to Beckenbauer. Breitner scored an important goal against Chile (1–0) another against Yugoslavia (2–0) and then converted the equalizing penalty during the final against Holland (2–1). Not bad for a full-back. The football world was at Beckenbauer's feet, but he kept an eye on the youngster, saying that with the talent he had and still so much time ahead of him he could take top spot. But Breitner couldn't put up with the Kaiser any more and left for Spain, turning his back on the national team. "I'll never return, however sure they are, it's not possible," he said. He won two league titles with Real Madrid (1975, 1976) and then, to everyone's surprise, returned to West Germany to play for Eintracht Brunswick. Although a wing-back when he left Germany, he was now playing in midfield. The following year, the prodigal child returned to the fold of Bayern Munich, straight in at the top. "The Kaiser", who used to scornfully call him "the intellectual", had left to play for Cosmos New York, so the position of Bayern skipper was vacant. Breitner became the play-maker, and called the shots on and off the pitch, securing the departure of coach Guyla Lorant. He won another two league titles (1980, 1981) and the German Cup (1982).

Mesmerized, a young man called Karl-Heinz Rummenigge learnt from him. The rookie would subsequently snatch the Golden Ball award from under the master's nose in 1981. "The Golden Ball I've no interest in it," was Breitner's unprompted response

"I don't want to be an example."

His autobiography, entitled *I Don't Want to Be an Example*, was published during the same period, making him new enemies. He revealed the salaries of players of the Bundesliga, for example. In support of his actions, he said: "We're under-paid because we are ranked in the category of performers. Breitner, Rolling Stones, Sophia Loren – same battle. The captains of German industry get paid much more than us. But we are forced to subject ourselves to abuse every Saturday and risk injury. I'm sure that if more people cast a cold and brutal eye over our profession, crises of hysteria could be avoided when the question of professional footballers' salaries was brought up for discussion."

The words caused a scandal, but Breitner pretended not to understand it. He had only told the truth. Later, on becoming a pundit on German television, much sought after on account of his straight talking, he admitted that his frankness created difficulties for him. "It's caused me a lot of problems. But I'm not afraid of problems."

In his book, the admirer of George Best spared no one. Not even referees, whom he judged to be mediocre and cowardly. "The day a referee says to me, 'Breitner, here's a yellow card for clambering on your opponent when he was preparing to head the ball', I'll respect referees."

Even more iconoclastic, he fought against the hypocrisy of denying that violence existed in football. "You have to learn how to foul. Football is a combat sport, more attacking than judo or karate. Football is like boxing. Contact is an everyday part of the game, sometimes combat is widespread. Anyone on the move or passing within reach is a target. Yet we're teaching lads a no-contact game. We should be telling them 'Foul him! Take his leg! Have him!' What I mean is that we should teach lads how to foul without putting the opponent at risk. Until the age of 18, we shout, 'Above all, no fouls!' They reach senior level with absolutely no idea how to stand up for themselves, and rush around with no control over their opponents."

Obviously, the press came in for criticism too, but without acrimony. Over the years, Western Germany's enfant terrible learned to accept certain truths. "I've had bad experiences with the press. Journalists are fantasists and make too much up. I had no time for anyone who published lies or distorted my statements. I had issues with the scandal press. Readers want to be lied to, they want sensationalism, even if it's not true. Some got it through me."

Although Breitner's book appeared shortly before his involvement in a second World Cup final in 1982, his main objective was to denounce the death of German footballing talent. "What's happened to our football? Run like mad, dig in, cover the pitch, fight, scrap. In 1972, Beckenbauer, Netzer and Gerd Muller were true talents. Today, it's Rummenigge, Hansi Muller and … and … no one else! 1980 European Champions? In 1972, Dietz, Allofs, Briegel and Cullmann would have had a guaranteed place … in front of the box!" He read out in public the names of the guilty parties, people with whom he had played. A bad team-mate to the last.

After retiring from the pitch, Breitner also retired from public life and donated his money to physically disabled children. An exemplary husband and already the father of two daughters, he adopted a mixed-race child. It was as if, underneath it all, the person tagged as a bad boy was a perfectly balanced human being, now distanced from the crazy world of football. ∎

the uncontrollable **geniuses!**

Éric Cantona

THE KING

the uncontrollable **geniuses!**

"I play against the idea of losing. Defeat is not a game."

Eric Cantona

The French call him "bad boy"; the English prefer "enfant terrible". Out of cautiousness and out of self-preservation, on each side of the Channel, we frequently choose to distance ourselves in translation by keeping to the original "Eric le rouge", "Cantona le rebelle" or even "Mad Eric". In terms of bad boys, the brooding-eyed Frenchman has a very plausible claim to the title of king, or at least of heir apparent to George Best.

Although born in Marseille on May 24, 1966, Eric Cantona was to come to England to seek love and recognition, after having done everything to ensure he'd never get this in France. But the bad boy make-up is such that they always need that little bit more adoration and support to keep them satisfied.

With his talent on the ball, Cantona was quickly spotted by a number of top-flight French clubs, even though he was still playing with his local club at Caillols, a suburb of Marseille. It was finally Auxerre that carried off the prize. "Canto" soon became the favourite of the iconic coach Guy Roux. He was the best in all the physical tests and was the one player who could decide the outcome of a match, taking the ball past all his opponents to score.

On November 5, 1983 he made his debut in the French premier division at the age of 18. The following season, he was loaned to Martigues in Division 2. On his return to Burgundy, he continued to progress and frequently earned the admiration of his opponents, sometimes even terrorizing his team-mates. The black eye sported one day by the international goalkeeper Bruno Martini when the French team were together was the souvenir of a dressing-room encounter with an unfriendly fist swung by a so-called friend. >

"I love you, I don't know why, but I love you."

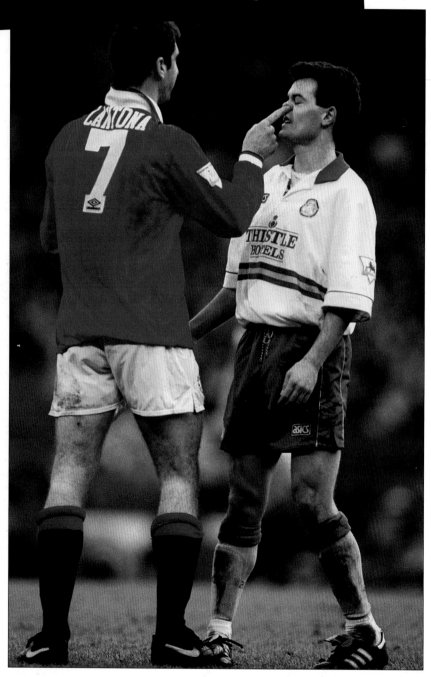

His bad behaviour was not seen on the public stage, however, until April 1988 at Nantes, where Cantona was guilty of a dangerous tackle on the Nantes player Michel Der Zakarian, which earned him a three-match suspension. Don't wind Canto up. He transferred to Marseille, but was not called up to the French squad by manager Henri Michel, whom he consequently called a "shitbag" in August 1989. In January 1989, during an Olympique Marseille friendly at Sedan, his coach, Gerard Gili, made the decision to bring him off. Leaving the pitch, Canto removed his shirt and threw it angrily to the ground.

He soon left Marseille, on loan to Montpellier where, in a corridor, he once again settled a dressing-room row with team-mate Jean-Claude Lemoult with his fists, before returning to Marseille. There was a reciprocal lack of trust between Cantona and Raymond Goethals, who had become coach in the meantime. "Football was going through strange times. Things happened that were judged subsequently," he would say later. He moved on to Nîmes. In December 1991, he insulted the members of a disciplinary committee ruling on his case after he threw a ball at a referee. The judges imposed a two-month suspension.

It was the end of Cantona's career in French football. He too announced his all too early retirement, but saw sense and accepted English club Sheffield Wednesday's offer of a trial period. He played in an exhibition match and signed five days later … for Leeds. Several weeks later, inspired by Cantona, Leeds won the League Championship. Delighted, he made declarations that enchanted the English fans: "I love you, I don't know why, but I love you." Spoken by Cantona, in his strong Marseille accent, this was asking to be made into a recording, and one fan seized the opportunity. The single worked its way up to the top of the charts.

The following season, on November 27, 1992, he signed for Manchester United. Although it seemed sudden, Cantona had, in fact, requested a transfer on two occasions. Yet another slanging match with Leeds manager Howard Wilkinson, who had consigned him, for once, to the bench, brought the Leeds/Cantona story to an end. Wilkinson's verdict on the Frenchman: "Eric is brilliant, but his style and personality don't fit with British football. >

"When seagulls follow a trawler, it is because they think sardines will be thrown into the sea!"

I spent more time talking to him than any other player. But I couldn't put up with his childish temperament. He won't do any better in Manchester. He'll never reach the heights of the likes of John Charles or Johnny Giles. Even the great players have a use-by date."

Cantona, who would now be simply "Eric the Red" and voted player of the century by Man Utd fans, maintained that he was the boss at Leeds and Wilkinson didn't have his say. "I entertained everyone. When they found out I was leaving, fans broke windows. But that's the way it is, I need change. It's in my nature. I need it more than others. I like to live in the moment. It's true of my game, my career and my life."

On the other side of the Pennines, Cantona found a new admirer in Alex Ferguson, manager of the Reds. "*Eric, c'est mon plaisir,*" the staunch Francophile told a dumbfounded gathering in French. Ferguson's son would even go on to study in Paris. Cantona then won a second English league title (he would end up with a total of five, in addition to two Cups). He was to play 143 matches and score 64 goals with Manchester United.

Having been called back up to the French squad from 1989, he developed as an international player under Gerard Houllier and then Michel Platini. Aime Jacquet, however, would have to do without his genius following yet another episode from the hot-headed "Mad Eric". On January 25, 1995, the man who appeared 45 times for his country and scored 19 goals, unleashed a spectacular kung-fu kick on a Crystal Palace fan who insulted him as he was leaving the pitch after being sent off for the fifth time in two years.

The images of this incredible incident spread like wildfire across the world. Guy Roux spoke with President Mitterrand's entourage to see whether French diplomacy could bring about a reduction of the two-week prison sentence imposed on the "Crazy Frenchie". This was finally commuted to a 120-day community service order, adapted specially to the English legal system for the occasion. His sporting suspension would last until October 1. Despite all this, Cantona was not completely shunned. Another bad boy, Vinnie Jones (see page 108), offered support in an equally spectacular fashion. "Eric did what so many of us would like to do. Fans can be dangerous and the police should sort out this serious problem."

The English press only scratched the surface of the Frenchman's behaviour. Nevertheless, the *Guardian* did pay him a sort of homage in a brave editorial: "Although the act of violence must be condemned, in the context, it can be understood. If half the indignation aroused by Cantona's behaviour had been spent on combating the filthy language from the stands, the incident would never have happened."

After the incident, more bewildering than ever, Cantona entertained a press conference with the memorable words: "When seagulls follow a trawler, it is because they think sardines will be thrown into the sea!" His statements caused a stir, as did the news that this wouldn't be the end of his career: "I play against the idea of losing. Defeat is not a game."

France would have to do without Cantona for the 1996 European Championship, but he would play again (and well). He ended his professional career in May 1997 with a final classic Cantona comparison: "A football club is like a fiancée. When you have nothing left to say to her, when you no longer want to share things with her, it is better to leave her, that's it!" he said.

Cantona then became a film producer and actor (*Le Bonheur est dans le Pré, L'Outremangeur* …). He was also responsible for selecting the French beach soccer team, which won the world championship in 2005. His strategy: "I try to find players who can run ten metres intelligently instead of running fifty like morons."

"Eric the King" reacted, in his own way, to another bad boy's appointment as coach of the French national team (see page 102). "Domenech or someone else, it makes no difference. The friend of a friend of a friend, they're all the same. They all bend over to let people give it to them." >

UXBRIDGE COLLEGE

LEARNING CENTRE

"I entertained everyone. When they found out I was leaving, fans broke windows. But that's the way it is, **I need change. It's in my nature.** I need it more than others. I like to live in the moment. It's true of my game, my career and my life."

The last provocation to date from the King is certainly not the most surprising, but none the less uncomfortable from the former captain of the French squad. Just before the 2006 World Cup, Cantona announced that he would be supporting England and not "les Bleus", arguing: "England is the country of football." Even though, as Cantona pointed out, at the end of the day none of that really interested him. His life had moved on. ■

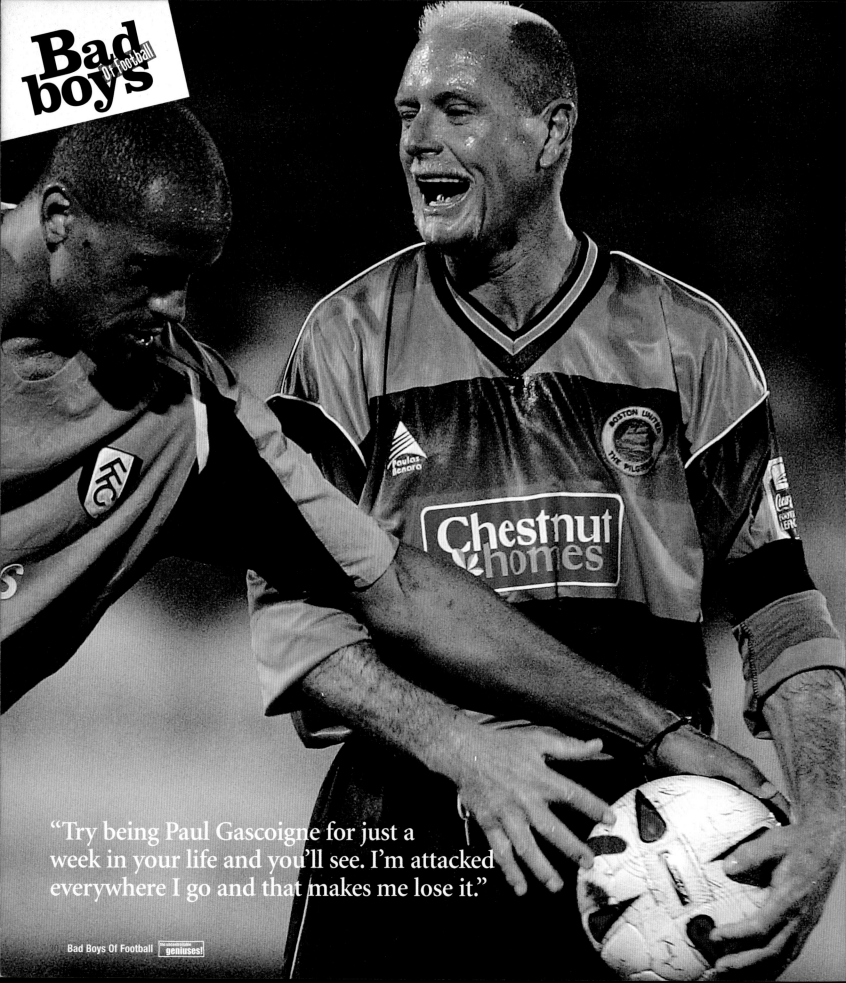

"Try being Paul Gascoigne for just a week in your life and you'll see. I'm attacked everywhere I go and that makes me lose it."

Paul Gascoigne

THIS BLOKE'S TOO MUCH!

the uncontrollable
geniuses!

Paul Gascoigne

Everything about Paul Gascoigne spells excess: his talent, his appetite, his weight, his drinking, his temper, his passion for football, his aversion to defeat, his contracts and his ties with his home, the tough city of Newcastle. It was there, at the age of 10, that he decided to become a professional footballer after winning a penalty shoot-out. From then on, his teachers were unable to keep him under control in class. "Unruly" was the kinder of the euphemisms used to describe his behaviour. John, his father, was unemployed, but always had the money for his boots. When "Gazza" was 13, he took him to all the junior trials in the region, and at Ipswich, Middlesbrough and Southampton, but it was finally with Newcastle, at the age of 16, that he first signed as an apprentice in 1983. That same evening, his father took him to the pub to celebrate.

When the international and future Marseille player Chris Waddle saw the newcomer run out for the first time, he laughed out loud. "I thought it was a joke. He was heavy, awkward. But, as soon as he had the ball at his feet, I understood why he was signed." The same comments were made by the iconic Kevin Keegan, who scornfully referred to him at first as "Red Legs".

Gazza was exceptionally gifted with the ball. Could he, though, pig out as much as he liked on chocolate bars or cream cakes? Just let the great Jack Charlton, who was briefly his manager at Newcastle, or even Kevin Keegan try and ask him! They would soon see the tempers the youngster was capable of flying into. Some of his team-mates were already predicting he would go down the same road as George Best.

For the time being, he quickly established himself as the Magpies' play-maker. He played 107 matches and scored 25 goals before being transferred to Tottenham in 1988 for two million pounds, a record for a 21-year-old player. The adult Paul would still sometimes cry like a child, and between 1990 and 1996 his tears would ensure him the love and indulgence of all England. In the 1990 World Cup semi-final against West Germany (1–1: Germany won 4–3 on penalties) in Italy, the tears flowed when he received a yellow card that he knew would rule him out of the final, if England made it, which was still a possibility at that point in the match. The entire country was in uproar. After England were knocked out, Margaret Thatcher, the Iron Lady, met and consoled the England squad and was hugged by Gazza. Shortly afterwards, he recorded the hit *Fog on the Tyne*, and was paid in the region of £10,000 for his interviews.

But his world crashed down when, in May 1991, he badly injured his right knee during a collision in the FA Cup Final against Nottingham Forest (2–1 after extra time). A grey year followed. Barely recovered from the operation, Paul returned to Dunston, the working-class area of Newcastle where he was born and where now he and Jimmy "Five Bellies" Gardner, his childhood friend turned on-the-scene bodyguard, caused fights and incidents in the bars and nightclubs. He was expecting to play again in January, but when he tore his cruciate ligament a second time, his season was over. >

"What do you want, I can't live my life shut away."

His transfer to Lazio Rome, already budgeted for approximately £6,000,000, was in doubt. Condemnation sprung up again for his drunken and violent behaviour when he was supposed to be convalescing in hospital. Gazza defended himself as best he could: "Try being Paul Gascoigne for just a week in your life and you'll see. I'm attacked everywhere I go and that makes me lose it. I want you to understand, I'm just like you. I don't use five-ply toilet paper and I don't bathe in milk."

Despite everything, Paul did discover Italy. One year earlier, on the pre-signature of his contract, seven thousand fans awaited him at the airport. In front of the Coliseum, he was ecstatic. "English fans were here recently by the looks of it?" But, this time, there was not much to enjoy, with just 47 matches and six goals in three years. His only amusement was belching in front of camera during interviews or dropping his shorts to photographers. He fought with paparazzi when he went out at night. In training, on April 7, 1994, he fractured the tibia of team-mate Alessandro Nesta. After three dismal seasons, he left Italy and returned north, where the flawless grounds and clumsy defenders made his crosses look better.

His move to Glasgow Rangers sparked a revival. Between 1995 and 1998 he became a platinum blonde, played 102 matches, scored 39 times and was voted 1996 footballer of the year in Scotland. Next came his marriage to Sheryl, divorcee and mother of two, who stood up to him like a strong-armed publican. The wedding, just before Euro 96 in England, was the height of bad taste, with television stars rubbing shoulders with some fairly seedy friends from Gazza's childhood.

At the top of his game, he took his preparations for the European Championship seriously. First, he taught his colleagues how to do the "dentist's chair": a player sits with his head tipped back while a colleague empties a bottle of something alcoholic down his throat. Then, on the flight home from the pre-tournament warm-up tour of Asia, he broke nearly £7,000 worth of fixtures when demonstrating kung-fu to his team-mates. He reasserted himself on the pitch with a superb goal in the first round against Scotland (2–0) and proved his worth. Then, during the penalty shoot-out in the semi-final in which England again lost to Germany (1–1, 6–5 on penalties), "Baby Paul" once again broke down in tears.

The rest is just a long and spluttering litany of the same stories: drinking binges, moments of genius, injuries, head-butts, disputes with his coaches. Short of form, Gazza once again courted controversy before the 1998 World Cup. His case divided the country. England manager Glenn Hoddle did everything he could to encourage Paul to make the necessary effort. He called him up for the preparatory matches, but Gazza couldn't run far and quickly ran out of breath. He confessed to smoking a pack of cigarettes a day. He was photographed, pint of beer in hand, with the singer Rod Stewart, and then in the street stuffing his face with a kebab dripping in grease. "What do you want, I can't live my life shut

away. I have a good lifestyle. I travel the world. I have great cars and enough put away at the bank. I only ask people to believe in me, I'll be ready for the World Cup," he protested at a press conference. However, he had lost Hoddle's trust and wasn't picked. This was "Gazzagate", and the snub was soon followed by another, when Gazza topped the list of least intelligent Brits in a survey published by *Focus* magazine.

The following season, at Middlesbrough and then at Everton, Paul Gascoigne finally attempted to tackle his alcohol problem. Only to go back to Newcastle and get legless again. He tried his luck in the United States … and failed. He played four matches in China, in 2002, with Gansu Tianma. In 2004 he tried for a player-manager position at Boston United in the Third Division. After two months, he announced that he had changed … his name! He would now be called "G8" (great with a Geordie accent). Over the same period, Sheryl lodged complaints of marital abuse.

2005 should have been the year of redemption. Gascoigne announced on TV that he was going to tackle his real problem – accept the fact that he was no longer the footballer he used to be and get his coaching badges. England cried in front of the box and forgave him everything. In October he started as manager of Kettering Town FC, a small club in the Northern Conference. He was sacked after 39 days … In December, Gazza was arrested again, this time for allegedly smacking a photographer in the face while attending a fund-raising event for a help centre for alcoholics and drug addicts …

The pit is bottomless, the story never-ending. ∎

Diego
Maradona
THE GREATEST OF ALL

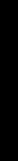

– What more do you want, when you're world champion, worshipped by the planet and father of two fantastic girls?
– To be loved even more!

the uncontrollable
geniuses!
Diego Maradona

When he was a child, some people thought he was a dwarf. When dad Diego presented his gifted, seven-year-old son to the coaches in the suburbs of Buenos Aires, they thought they were dealing with a kid with growth problems, an initial misunderstanding that was never really rectified for "El Pibe" ("the kid"). At the age of 12, he was already a star and was trawled around everywhere. He made his debut in the First Division at 16 with Argentinos Juniors. Although he was shy, it wasn't a good idea to wind him up. Hugo Gatti, goalkeeper of Boca Juniors, called him *gordito* ("little fattie") at the start of the match. Maradona scored four goals and afterwards left the pitch with his chin jutting out and head held high.

It was obvious to everyone that this was an extraordinary player. His future was in Europe. From 1979, the top clubs were interested in the player. The Argentine dictatorship, however, forced their most valuable PR asset to remain in the country until 1982. Without fear of the possible reprisals for him and his family, Maradona clamoured to be allowed to go to Barcelona. He squared up to Guillermo Suarez Mason, manager of Argentinos Juniors and an associate of the military regime.

At the end of 1981, Boca Juniors stepped up the number of matches to show off their prodigy. Maradona broke down. "I can't do it any more, I don't want to play any more." He was 21 years old. After getting back into his stride, he had to wait until the 1982 World Cup to secure his exit pass. He was announced as one of the future heroes of the World Cup in Spain. He was, in fact, irresistible during the first group phase, notably scoring two goals against Hungary (4–1). In the second group phase, Argentina faced Brazil and Italy. Against the Azurri, he was closely marked by the abrasive Claudio Gentile. Sheer agony! Italy won 2–1, and Maradona was sick to the stomach. >

In the following match, against Brazil (3–1), he avenged a team-mate with a powerful kick to a Brazilian player's lower stomach and was given a red card. It was the end of his World Cup.

Transferred to Barcelona for $8 million, he was welcomed as a hero. He played 58 matches and scored 38 goals. Identified by all the defenders of the Liga as the danger man to be brought down, he was subjected to one aggressive act after another, in a league and an era in which players received hardly any protection at all.

Right at the start of the 1983–84 season, having just won his first title in Europe, the 1983 Spanish Cup (2–1 against Real Madrid in the final), he sustained a terrible ankle fracture, inflicted on him by Andoni Goicoechea, "the butcher of Bilbao", chief hatchet man in a team passionate about rough play. Maradona was to be absent from the pitch for 106 days, only returning to competitive action in 1984. At the end of the season, Barcelona reached the Spanish Cup Final again, losing 1–0 to Atletico Bilbao. Under attack again, he lost his cool at the final whistle and instigated a mass brawl. Already high on cocaine, he went for his aggressors, studs flying, like a madman. He was suspended, but a timely royal pardon from King Juan Carlos meant that he would remain, for the time being, a stranger to the judicial system. Maradona was worth his weight in gold, more than a mere coach. When he clashed with German Udo Lattek, who reproached him for his nocturnal outings while the coach stayed in to discuss his tactical choices, it was the German who lost his job. These two seasons also gave him time to clash with his president, Jose Luis Nunez, and to experience a turbulent love affair with the Catalan media. In the summer of 1984, the romance ended.

Next came another love affair, this time with disfavoured Naples, which welcomed the most fantastic and whimsical of football geniuses with open arms. For the Neapolitans it was the perfect way to thumb their noses at the richest and most titled clubs in the world. For seven years, in the south of Italy, Maradona experienced his golden years, loved, finally, for his game and for himself, and not for what he brought in. Meanwhile he was detested in the rest of Italy, especially the north, by those who had missed out on the opportunity to sign him. During Maradona's first match for Naples outside the region, in Verona, a banner was unfurled for the Argentinian by anti-southern *tifosi*, saying "Welcome to Italy".

Until 1991, Diego of Naples would experience a passionate love affair with this city, where they recited special prayers: "Our Maradona, who descends on the pitch, hallowed be thy name. Naples is thy kingdom, deliver us from delusion and lead us to the league title."

He was loved; but, above all, he was in love. A Zorro with studs, he had already made a number of left-wing statements: "I grew up in a deprived

neighbourhood. Deprived of water, deprived of light, deprived of the telephone." "If people have both hands up, I like to put them straight. If they have both hands down, I prefer to help them."

He played on the muddy fields of villages to raise funds for a sick child. He went into action to double the bonuses of his team-mates. In 1987 he gave his club the title, the famous *Scudetto*, snatched from under the noses of Berlusconi's AC Milan and Giovanni Agnelli's Juventus. In 1988 he was the top scorer of the Calcio with 15 goals. In 1989 he won the UEFA Cup, after Naples knocked Juve out in the quarter-finals (0–2, 3–0 after extra time) and made a mockery of Bayern Munich in the semi-finals (2–0, 2–2). Maradona even scored in the final against Stuttgart (2–1, 3–3). He was at the height of his career. In 1990 he married Claudia, his childhood sweetheart back in Argentina, and became Italian league champion for the second time.

Meanwhile, in 1986, he won the World Cup with Argentina in Mexico. In the quarter-finals, he scored the infamous punched goal against England (2–0). "It was the Hand of God," he commented, acknowledging his action de facto, which he saw as avenging his people for the hammering defeat four years earlier at the hands of the UK forces in the Falkland Islands. Diego of Argentina had no shame and did not justify himself. His second goal spoke for itself. In a piece of play totalling 37 paces, Maradona left his half, took the ball past six opponents and beat the goalkeeper Peter Shilton. Bobby Robson, the English manager, was inspired to pay tribute. "His second goal was fantastic. I don't like him, but I admire him!"

It seemed "Dieguito" could do anything. He was already overweight, but no one dared say anything when he ordered pizzas at 4 a.m. Granted an audience with the Pope, he had the temerity to complain to the Holy Father that the rosary beads he was given were the same as those handed out to everyone else. He lived by day and by night. He lived to excess, too fast, too high, too hard. Already hooked on cocaine, he lost control of his career, his affairs, his whole life. Ruined in 1985 by his agent, Jorge Cysterpiller, the player turned instead to Guillermo Coppola. This former bank employee, now an agent and confidant of footballers, guided him on his long Neapolitan night (he would end up in prison in 1997). In 1986 Maradona had to deal with a paternity suite, having refused to acknowledge the son of Cristina Sinagra. A court would later force him to do so. >

"I promised not to cry"

Naples is a funny kind of city, and you run into funny people. In 1989, after the Copa America, the South American cup of nations, he stayed in Brazil for two months before returning to Italy. It was said that he was being threatened by the Camorra, the local mafia. The 1990 World Cup would seal the divorce. An irony of sorts, for it was in Naples that Argentina played its semi-final against Italy (winning 1–1, 4–3 on penalties). For the first time ever, Maradona was booed in the San Paolo stadium. "*Hijos de Putas!*" was his response, during the Italian national anthem, to all the Italians from the north who had come to shout him down. Argentina won the semi-final, but Maradona lost the support of the people. At the final, in Rome, constant booing filled the Olympic Stadium. The Italians sided with the Germans. For the entire game, Maradona was marked aggressively by Guido Buchwald and saw very little of the ball. In the 85th minute, the Argentinians, down to ten men after Monzon was sent off, conceded a harsh penalty and lost 1–0. When receiving the runners-up prize, amid a storm of heckles from the crowd, Maradona broke down in tears. "This is the biggest disappointment of my career. I am sad, bitter and furious."

What followed was an endless litany of incidents, as he descended into 15 years of hell. First his coke addiction, which began in Barcelona. "I was 22 years old and I thought I was smart. You can never say you're cured, it's a life-long battle. At the beginning, the drug makes you euphoric, as if you've won the league. Then, you say to yourself, 'Who cares about tomorrow if I'm a champion today?'" On April 26, 1991, Maradona tested positive at Naples. He left Italy, where he received a 14-month prison sentence, in absentia, for cocaine consumption and trafficking.

He had not long arrived back in Buenos Aires when he was arrested for the same offence. He left for Spain and signed for FC Sevilla, where he made his debut on October 4, 1992. A series of wasted opportunities and disappointments followed. This same season, he lost his paternity suit. He left the club in May 1993 and returned to Argentina, where he would play for Newell's Old Boys.

But he was caught in a vicious circle. Hounded by the press, at times he gave in, putting on a ridiculous show, or tried to shake them off displaying a total lack of sense. In January 1994, he fired on reporters with a compressed-air rifle. He then worked towards the goal of the 1994 World Cup in the United States. He began to train more seriously, lost weight and appeared, honed, at the World Cup. He scored during Argentina's first match against Greece (4–0). He rushed in front of a camera, mad-eyed and grimacing like the Devil, an eternal recurrence. When he took a drug test four days later, after their victory against Nigeria (2–1), he tested positive for ephedrine.

Maradona left the World Cup more demoralized than ever. "I promised not to cry," he said, making sure he didn't give in to the temptation. As he gradually fell apart, a journalist friend and writer asked him, "But what more do you want, when you're world champion, worshipped by the planet and father of two fantastic girls?" The tormented soul's response: "To be loved even more!"

Maradona foundered, but then returned to the game, with Boca Juniors in 1996. He dyed his hair the colours of the club and then Venetian blonde. It wasn't him, and he became systematically provocative. On each goal scored by his team, he kissed his team-mate Caniggia on the mouth. He put on weight and lost his way. He missed five penalties that season, one after the other. >

"I spoke to God and he asked me to stay quiet."

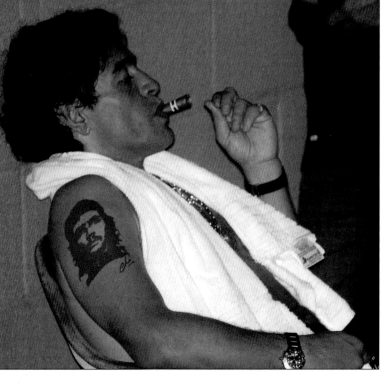

At the same time, his friend, former world champion Alberto Tarantini, who was now working in public relations for a nightclub, was arrested twice in six months for "possession of cocaine". Until this point, Maradona's agent, Guillermo Coppola, had not been caught in the act. He was said to be protected by Argentina's populist leader, President Carlos Menem, elected in May 1995, who kept in with Maradona, still the people's idol. "El Pibe" spoke back. "Nothing could stop me criticizing the government when I see what's happened in my country. If I've drawn closer to Carlos Menem, it's only because I sympathized with his grief as a father when his son was killed in a helicopter accident."

In 1997, at 37 years of age, Maradona was still playing for Boca. He was out of shape, but called on former sprinter Ben Johnson, who had been suspended for doping offences, to revitalize him. The training sessions in the pampas were filmed. When Maradona scored his 150th goal in Argentina's league championship, he gripped the bars of the stadium, with haggard eyes, like a furious animal. On October 25, 1997, he played his last match with Boca against River Plate, after testing positive for cocaine, although this was circumvented in the short term by a piece of legal ingenuity. Two overdoses followed in January 2000 and April 2004. The first led Maradona to seek refuge in Cuba with Fidel Castro, who looked after and cared for him. Claudia was also there. She placed his affairs in order, fired Coppola and watched over her husband, even though she no longer lived with him. In 1999 Maradona was forced to acknowledge a young daughter in Argentina, fruit of his relations with waitress Valeria Sabalain.

Thanks to a gastric band, he finally managed to reduce his weight and keep it down. Apparently off the drug, he returned to Argentina in 2005, where he became a television host. His show, *La Noche del 10*, was a hit. El Pibe put on a show, danced, played ball and had reconciliations with old rivals. Pele appeared on the show and put an end to their age-old quarrel as to who was the best player in the world. Although Maradona never missed an opportunity to claim he was lucky in life because he could have been "a worse player than Pele", this time Maradona asked the people of Argentina, who were glued to their televisions, "Which of us was the better player? My mother thinks it's me, but Pele's mum thinks otherwise." An intelligent way to close the debate. Argentina melted before this reformed scoundrel who declared his undying love to his wife. She didn't give in to the public overtures, but nevertheless drew closer to her man.

During the 2006 World Cup in Germany, Maradona managed to support the Argentina team without feeling compelled to steal the show from the players of the day, contenting himself with a few photos and television images. El Pibe's cheeky explanation of his change: "I spoke to God and he asked me to stay quiet." Was this the humour of a man who had at last found peace after years of immense suffering? Jorge Valdano, one of Argentina's 1986 World Champions, put forward the following explanation: "Without the ball, Maradona is just a man incapable of living up to his perfect memory."

Perhaps... But there are many sides to Maradona, sincere and untruthful, inspirational and deceitful, captivating and disarming, and capable of summing up his passion with charming naivety: "The pull of football is as strong as loving your mum." ■

Lothar
Matthaeus
THE UNBENDING ONE

"I have no intention of letting anyone tread on my toes. Everyone should know who I am and what I want!"

Lothar Matthaeus

For a long time, Lothar Matthaeus believed that he wasn't on the pitch to be loved. He even believed the opposite. His father, caretaker of the Herzogenaurach Puma plant, in the suburbs of Nuremberg, taught him that he had to fight to win his place in the sun. So as a child Lothar did lap after lap of the pitch with gritted teeth, until he became an extraordinary athlete. In the summer of 1979, during his first training session with the professionals at Borussia Moenchengladbach, the 18-year-old Matthaeus set about getting noticed, running his heart out and tackling hard. Too hard for the likes of Berti Vogts, who knew all about that. At the end of the session, the master took the rookie aside to teach him about respect for elders. The kid's response: "I have no intention of letting anyone tread on my toes. Everyone should know who I am and what I want!"

A year later, he made the team for the first time. He came on to the pitch against Holland (3–2), about 20 minutes from the end, to mark a certain Johan Cruyff. But Lothar was not there to admire the giant. He had just taken part, as boss of Borussia's midfield, in the two-match final of the UEFA Cup against Eintracht Frankfurt (3–2, 0–1). Whatever Vogts thought, the youngster was already the team boss, a tireless, born leader who abhorred defeat as much as mediocrity.

The two men would meet again 15 years later, in 1994, when Berti Vogts would become manager of Germany's national side, from which Matthaeus would be dropped. "Vogts never trusted me because I had an excellent relationship with a journalist and he didn't like it." Lothar was, in fact, suspected of being a mole for the top-selling daily *Bild*. During the deplorable performance of the Germans during the 1994 World Cup in the United States, internal management discussions, often lively ones, were reported, at length, in *Bild*. Jurgen Klinsmann and Thomas Helmer would be the accusers.

Without Lothar, Germany would win the 1996 European Championships. But, faced with a ton of injuries, Vogt called him up as sweeper during the 1998 World Cup, declaring: "You can write that I ate my hat. Only the result counts." But, in 1998, the 1990 world champions were spent. They were knocked out in the quarter-finals by Croatia (3–0). Worse was to come in 2002, at the European Championship, when the same team, or almost the same, but now coached by Erich Ribbeck, a close friend of Matthaeus, would not even make it past the first round. It was the end of an era and the last of the 150 caps won by "der Lothar", as the Germans called him. Although they love to burn their idols, on this occasion the Germans forgave Matthaeus his undignified exit. Over the years, they learned to love him, despite everything.

In 1984, however, Lothar Matthaeus had shocked them by revealing a sensational transfer to Bayern Munich. After turning down the DM 50,000 (approximately £17,500) offered personally by Jupp Heynckes, the Moenchengladbach coach, who considered him his spiritual son and was absolutely intent on him staying, he missed a penalty against his future team during the German Cup final. Bayern won the trophy (1–1, 7–6 on penalties). Unconcerned, Lothar moved on to Bavaria, where he strung together three league titles. He even managed to persuade his new club, historically linked to Adidas, to let him play in Puma.

In Munich, he soon clashed with Soren Lerby. The Dane left for Monaco. "I've never felt like a boss, but my heart and my pride are equal to anything," commented Lothar laconically. All he had to say about his then coach, Jupp Derwall, was "He hasn't really helped me to become established." >

"It is Lothar Matthaeus who decides his destiny"

He became captain of the German squad under manager Franz Beckenbauer, then left Germany for Italy and Inter Milan in 1988. The German people were cold-shouldered by the player they had finally come to adulate. "In Italy," he said, "I've gone further and I've become stronger." His coach, Giovanni Trapattoni, who thought he had the look of a wild beast, offered him the No. 10 shirt, even though he'd never dared wear anything other than No. 8 in the defensive midfield. "I want you to become as vital as Platini or Maradona," said "the Trap".

He would be, in his own way: in terms of power, will, fierce determination and iron lungs. He won trophies too: the Italian league title in 1989, the 1991 UEFA Cup and the 1990 World Cup. Germany's triumph in the Olympic Stadium in Rome was only marred by the Italian and German crowd's regrettable booing of Maradona, the only footballer ever revered by Matthaeus, but whom he brought down 1–0. During the 1986 World Cup final, lost by Germany (3–2) at the Aztec Stadium in Mexico, Lothar did not think twice before viciously tackling "El Pibe de

Oro" from behind in the 23rd minute. Nevertheless, with Maradona's free-kick that followed, the Argentines opened the scoring.

Returning in 1992 to a Bayern now managed by Beckenbauer, Matthaeus considered himself a candidate for captain, but there were strong characters above him such as "Kalle" (Karl-Heinz Rummenigge) and Beckenbauer himself. He also had Uli Hoeness to deal with and, on the pitch, Mehmet Scholl. The continual conflicts and rows were manna from heaven for *Bild*, the German daily, which was only too glad to cash in on the escapades at Bayern, nicknamed "FC Hollywood". Once Matthaeus got more than he bargained for when Bixente Lizarazu, the hot-blooded Basque, gave him a good slap to show him who he was dealing with. The story not only made the front page the following day, but spread across the world. Star among stars, captain among captains, Matthaeus, already well into his thirties, felt unappreciated. "They don't respect me", "I feel alone", "Uli Hoeness has had no proper knowledge of the game for twenty years." These are snippets of a long series of complaints from Matthaeus. In 1999, at 37 years of age, he was voted the Bundesliga's player of the year, and was in the Bayern side that lost the Champions League final 2–1 to Manchester United, conceding two goals in time added on at the end of 90 minutes.

He then signed with the New York Metro Stars. "It is Lothar Matthaeus who decides his destiny," he loved to repeat, taking pleasure in speaking about himself in the third person, while discreetly observing the effect this had on the people he was speaking to. "Lothar wants to control everything. He even wants to choose the menus," said Erich Ribbeck when he was coach of the German national side.

In 2000, before ending his career as a European player, Lothar Matthaeus was finally given recognition. The German Federation, the DRB, offered him a testimonial at his favoured Munich stadium, against the national team. For the occasion, he made up with all his old football enemies, who were invited to the event. On the pitch, a revered 130-kilo hulk, Diego Maradona, even made an appearance and entertained the Olympic Stadium with some ball-juggling tricks. Happy, relaxed and rather surprised to finally be the star of the show, Matthaeus let slip a few tears, but only once he was alone in the dressing-room.

He became a coach in 2002 with Austrian side Rapid Vienna, but after disappointing results he moved on to Partizan Belgrade. In 2003, although he had just taken his club through Champions League qualification, he suddenly quit the job and later became the Hungarian coach. This was a safe position, and he filled it with an obvious pleasure and affability that was so unusual for this man whom the Germans nicknamed "the Unbending". He then left quietly to coach in Brazil and then at Salzburg, in peaceful Austria, in the shadow of Trapattoni, the much-publicized manager. After so many bad-tempered years in football, it was as if he was finally persuaded that his life wasn't just one long battle. ∎

"I wouldn't be any good if it wasn't for my mean nature."

Hristo Stoichkov

THE MAD DOG

Hristo Stoïtchkov was given his first nickname, "the Dog", well before he achieved his notoriety as a footballer. It was in Plovdiv, his home town of Bulgaria during the 1970s, an era when the Eastern bloc still seemed unshakeable. This already irascible kid had, according to legend, bitten a dog! In actual fact, in a particularly bad temper one day, he had used his teeth to puncture a ball. The frantic desire to win seemed insatiable in young Hristo. At 10 years of age, in Maritsa Plovdiv, he suffered a chest cramp and fainted on the pitch at Levski Sofia. While his coach was substituting him, he came to and burst into tears. In order to stay on the pitch, he announced that he would score – and, of course, he did.

Other nicknames were to follow: "the Dagger", "the Kurd", "El Bulgaro", all of which conveyed a fearsome shadow, a latent danger – an impression reinforced by his massive frame, stocky body and short, fighter's arms. With Stoichkov, no one was safe from a stunning dribble, a memorable rage, a sudden clout, a deadly retaliation or a hurled shirt. A brilliant striker, he is one of these people who can't tolerate indifference, who would die rather than languish in anonymity, be sidelined rather than stay silent. Like a fearless stand-up comedian, happy to cause offence for the sake of a laugh, Stoichkov was capable of self-destructing on and off the pitch, preferring the absurdity of an untenable situation to stooping so low as to compromise with the opponent.

As a military commander he would have been an impressive hero, capable of spectacular and unexpected breakthroughs, or a futile conqueror, responsible for terrible bloodshed in vain combat, persuaded that his talent, his intelligence and his will would always get him out of any situation. As a footballer, it was this self-belief that took him to the heights: fourth place with Bulgaria at the 1994 World Cup, the Golden Ball, four Spanish league titles (1991, 1992, 1993, 1994), the European Cup (1992) and the European Cup-Winners Cup (1997) with Barcelona. "Yes, I do have an impossible nature," he once admitted, "but this is my strength. Stoichkov is a complete

package. "I wouldn't be any good if it wasn't for my mean nature. When I go for it, I go all out." And he didn't worry about the consequences.

At the age of 18, he was an electrician but, more importantly, decisive attacker of CSKA Sofia, and had already built a reputation as a moaner, which his talent on the pitch barely took the edge off. He did everything he could to be noticed and respected, always pushing things to breaking point.

Hristo Stoichkov

Once, after an exhausting training session under Georgi Dimitrov, a CSKA coach well known for his inflexibility, he called out to the coach, in front of his dumbfounded team-mates, "Say Jacky, pass the towel!" Anyone else would have been dropped permanently from the team, but not Hristo, because he was already too important to the club. Encouraged by this, the following year, during the 1985 Bulgarian Cup final between CSKA and Levski, he started a mass brawl, even though his team were leading 2–1, and carried on the argument to the dressing-rooms. The two clubs were dissolved and five players, including Stoichkov, were suspended for life. In Bulgaria, before the fall of the Berlin wall, not even rebels messed with authority. You only got away with it if you were indispensable to the system. Stoichkov was pardoned less than a year later. The greats have impunity, for we owe them more than they owe us. Or so they are led to believe … >

> "I can often be buddy-buddy with my supposed sporting enemies."

Armed with this certainty, Stoichkov did nothing to tone down his act after transferring to Barcelona in 1990. In 1992 he became the first Bulgarian in history to win a European title, and his trademark rages, angry gesticulations, false hostility, coarse intimidation and the scornful raising of the arm when leaving the pitch were now known throughout Europe.

On a day-to-day basis, it was now Johan Cruyff Stoichkov was dealing with. Their relations were stormy, but the Dutch coach managed to integrate the mad dog individualist into an innovative formation, combining him perfectly with the Brazilian Romario. Semi-finalist and top scorer, with six goals, in the 1994 World Cup, Stoichkov was at the top of his game, and more provocative than ever. When Maradona was convicted of ephedrine doping during the World Cup, Hristo tried, in vain, to call him and offer comfort, with the argument: "I can often be buddy-buddy with my supposed sporting enemies."

At Barca, however, Cruyff could no longer put up with the mood swings of his star and forced him to quit Catalonia for Italy. This marked the start of his sporting decline. At Parma he played few games but had lots to say, and his language became even more aggressive. On his return to Barca, as a substitute, he set about the simple task of winding up the implacable Dutch coach Louis Van Gaal and, even more so, half of his team.

In 1996, during the European Championship in England, he overstepped the mark by fighting with all the Bulgarian directors, whom he accused, in no uncertain terms, of making cheese-paring economies by lodging the team in an old lunatic asylum with dilapidated equipment.

When, after the European Championship, his mentor, manager Dimitar Penev, was ousted, Stoichkov decided to quit the team and jeered at Penev's successor, Hristo Bonev: "Him? Don't know him. He's Mr Nobody." Later, however, to get back into his good books in the lead-up to the 1998 World Cup, Stoichkov personally came to his house to deliver a bouquet of flowers for his wife. The France campaign nevertheless proved to be bitterly disappointing for the Bulgarians, who were beaten by Nigeria (1–0) and then by Spain (6–1!) and failed to qualify from their group. When Stoichkov left he was murderous. The following year, at home in Sofia in his last appearance for his country, on June 9, 1999 against England (1–1), Stoichkov's *pièce de resistance* was to wear a captain's armband in the Catalan colours.

At the age of 34, after trying out adventures in Saudi Arabia and then in Japan (he left the latter country right in the middle of his contract), he moved to the United States and began to calm down. He played for three years in Chicago, and then in Washington, as player-manager, until December 2003, when he ended his playing career. Finally at peace, and with nothing more to prove, he began passing his football genius on to others – first to the youngsters at his club, then to the Bulgarian youth team and, in July 2004, to the Bulgarian national team, to which he became head coach. ∎

FIFA

Zinedine
Zidane
IN BLUE AND SEEING RED

"I've changed. I know there's no place for illegal knee-jerk reactions at this level of the competition any more. If I do the same thing at the World Cup, there will be serious consequences."

JUNE 1998

the geniuses!

Zinedine Zidane

"When you have such a strong desire to succeed, it sometimes leads to, let's say … differences."

"I went off the rails and I regret it. I was insulted, mocked and I reacted badly." These are the words of Zinedine Zidane, obviously. They were spoken on 18 September … 1993. Zidane was then playing at Bordeaux and, facing Marseille (who won 3–1) at the peak of the French league title race, he reacted badly under the pressure inflicted on him by the already experienced Marcel Desailly. The result: a punch in the face of his future French team-mate, a black eye and two stitches. A reaction that the great Marcel had never anticipated, one he'd never forget, and one he'd make no bones about recalling after July 9, 2006.

In 1993 Zidane was 22 years of age. This was simply an error of youth. Well, that's what Zizou said. "It's just learning the hard way, I take full responsibility." It wasn't enough to make him a bad boy, but, two years later, Zizou was at it again. The Girondins were playing the second leg of the final of the Intertoto Cup, a qualifier for the first round of the UEFA Cup, against Karlsruhe. After being caught by Thorsten Fink, Zidane slapped him in the face, even though Bordeaux were leading 2–0, after their 2–0 first-leg victory. He was sent off in the 24th minute. This was the painful beginning of Bordeaux's epic march to the final of the 1995–96 Cup Winners' Cup. "What I did was inexcusable, but I was constantly under attack," he claimed. Two months later, however, Zidane lost it again with a savage tackle on

Frederic Mendy during a Martigues–Bordeaux encounter (3–1) in Division 1. This was his third sending-off in two years. He was also sent off against Juventus, when a number of wicked tackles and stray fists resulted in an early shower; against Perouse (2–1) in September 1996, and then against Parma (0–1) five monthslatter. Was it just pressure? No, there was definitely something of the bad boy in this Zidane. His coach at the time supported him, but noted that "Zizou has fallen into the provocation trap." This clear-sighted coach was Marcello Lippi, the future manager of the 2006 World Cup winners.

In the lead-up to the World Cup hosted by France in 1998, Zidane seemed very nervous during the friendly warm-up matches. Against Finland (1–0), on June 5, 1998, he stamped on the chest of Jarkko Wiss. He received only a yellow card, but his captain, Didier Deschamps, and coach, Aime Jacquet, warned him about his temperament. Zidane was reassuring. "I've changed. I know there's no more room for illegal knee-jerk reactions at this level of the competition any more. If I do the same thing at the World Cup, there will be serious consequences."

But just as a bee, when provoked, can't help but sting, even if it perishes as a result, it's in the nature of the bad boy, in the heat of the moment, to ignore the consequences of his actions. Thus, in spite of the warning, Zidane snapped once again during the World Cup. Even

though France were leading Saudi Arabia 2–0 (final score 4–0), he stamped on the side of Fouad Amin, who had just made an unsuccessful attempt to tackle him. "His behaviour was premeditated," asserted the Saudi player. "He'd lost it. How can a great player of Zidane's calibre be allowed to cynically bring an opponent down? This accumulation of red cards for Zidane is, without doubt, due to his temperament." The Frenchman responded: "When you have such a strong desire to succeed, it sometimes leads to, let's say … differences."

But Zizou had not yet perfected his technique. In October 1998, in the Calcio, he received yet another red card against Inter (1–0). The same thing happened a year later, this time against Roma (1–0), for simulation. In the autumn of 2000, however, he surpassed himself. Having won the European Championship, Zidane was tipped for the Golden Ball award. On September 2, in a friendly with England (1–1), he retaliated after being marked tightly by dyed-in-the-wool bad boy Dennis Wise (see p. 90). Roger Lemerre, the manager, took him off before the yellow card turned red. On September 26 in the Champions League against La Coruna (0–0), he clattered into Emerson with a two-footed tackle. But his *coup de grâce* was one month later, against Hamburg (who won 3–1), when he callously head-butted Jochen Kientz, who was ruthlessly marking him. Sent off for the second time in four Division 1 matches, he blew any chance of

the Golden Ball and was suspended for five matches. "I deserved to be punished because what I did was illegal," admitted Zidane, defending himself half-heartedly, "but I want people to be aware of the facts leading up to what I did. The treatment inflicted on me by my opposite number made me especially angry. I'm sure he kneed me in the back deliberately." He added, "I'm a father and my behaviour should be exemplary."

For four years, Zizou did as he was told. At Real Madrid, he notched up not even one sending-off – until the second leg of the semi-final of the Spanish Cup, played away at FC Sevilla (0–1, 2–0 after the first leg), on February 11, 2004. Unbeknownst to the referee, after being elbowed by Pablo Alfaro, Zidane retaliated with a humiliating little slap. Unfortunately for the Galactico, the linesman saw everything – and off he went!

After being sent off again in 2004 as Real lost 2–0 to La Coruna, he kept his nose clean for a year. Real, however, dipped in the league and didn't win again in the Champions League. Time passed for Zidane, and titles became fewer and farther between. A movie would be made of him, based on one match, and one match alone. On April 23, 2005, Santiago-Bernabeu was crammed with ultra-sophisticated cameras installed by two film-makers, Douglas Gordon and Philippe Parreno. >

Bad boys

> **"We always talk about the retaliation. It obviously has to be punished. What I did can't be pardoned. But, if there is no provocation, there is no retaliation. The guilty party is the person who provokes the incident."**

Months of work, an entire team of artists and technicians for just one performer, Zinedine Zidane. In the final minute of the game, when he violently shoved an opponent, was he only thinking about helping out team-mate Raul in a skirmish? The thirteenth red card of his career was immortalized in *Zidane, a Portrait of the XXI Century*, which was on general release a year later. It was not, however, the most spectacular card.

One year later, thanks to his timely return to the French team, along with Lilian Thuram and Claude Makelele, Zidane played his last World Cup, in Germany. For some months France had looked solid but unattractive, and they would have to raise their game during the competition if they wanted to shine. The first matches (0–0 against Switzerland, 1–1 against South Korea) were poor, worrying even. Nervous, Zidane was cautioned in the match against Switzerland for taking a free-kick too quickly. Five days later, having been dominated throughout the match, Korea equalized in the 81st minute. Three minutes later, a group gathered just inside the Korean box. Zidane strode several yards to shove a Korean player. He received his second yellow card in two matches and would be unable to play in the decisive match against Togo (2–0). Domenech took him off almost immediately. Zidane left the pitch without so much as a glance at his coach.

Dazzling in the quarter-finals against Brazil (1–0), faultless and scoring (a penalty) against Portugal in the semi-finals (1–0), he then played in the World Cup final against Italy, the last match of his career. After he scored in the seventh minute with his "Panenka style" penalty against Gianluigi Buffon, Italy's response came off the head of Marco Materazzi just after the quarter-of-an-hour mark (1–1). Zidane seemed very upset by the fouls on Thierry Henry and Fabio Cannavaro's charges on Patrick Vieira. Yet the Argentine referee, Mr Elizondo, only penalized Zidane once for a foul. Extra time came and was dominated by France. The Italians, exhausted, retreated into their penalty area. Now it was possible that France could win its second World Cup and Zidane could pull off the craziest of feats in this, his last match. In the 104th minute, from a Willy Sagnol pass into the box, he headed a

powerful ball under the bar, but Buffon somehow managed to tip it over, a breathtaking save. Four minutes later Zidane and Materazzi exchanged words, out of sight of the referee. The Frenchman walked away and then, suddenly, retraced his steps and head-butted Materazzi right in the chest. There was no faking by Materazzi as he slumped to the ground in obvious distress. Head-butt, head-butt! Again Mr Elizondo saw nothing, but his assistant, Mr Luis Medina Cantalejo, told him all he needed to know. Sent off! His fourteenth red card. Twice as many as Gennaro Gattuso who – in the great tradition of the

brotherhood of bad boys (see page 66) – went over to comfort the Frenchman before he left the pitch.

When interviewed on Canal+ on July 13, Zidane apologized to his children and coaches, but he maintained that he did not regret his action. He had responded to provocation. "We always talk about the retaliation. It obviously has to be punished. What I did can't be pardoned. But, if there is no provocation, there is no retaliation. The guilty party is the person who provokes the incident." Undoubtedly a bad boy to the last. ■

Bad boys Of Football

Nicolas Anelka

José Luis Chilavert

Luis Fernandez

Gennaro Gattuso

Oliver Kahn

Jens Lehmann

Ahmed Hossam, aka Mido

Stuart Pearce

Jean-Marie Pfaff

Fabrizio Ravanelli

Wayne Rooney

Dennis Wise

the wind-up kings !!

They need their heads banging together. They're exasperating. They moan, argue and constantly try and bend the rules. These are all good players, obviously, but they're always up to their necks in dirty tricks, always coming out with killer remarks or bad language. They're incorrigible winners, natural born pests. But why do they have a place among the great names of football? Why do we remember a Gennaro Gattuso, a Luis Fernandez or a Jose Luis Chilavert? They know how to make themselves unbearable, wind up their team-mates and drive their coaches to distraction (and sometimes their players, if the wind-up kings themselves become coaches). True, but without them, would teams have the same appeal, would winning matches come so easily?

They aren't strictly the geniuses or butchers that their teams just can't do without, but, in their own way, they get on with the dirty job of chipping away at their opponents, drumming it into them that they'll never, ever give in. Harassers par excellence, insatiable braggers and never satisfied, these bad boys are the Grumpy Young Men of football, and the big teams need them. They're the key players who unrelentingly punish mistakes and grab their chances, showing no mercy when opponents lose concentration or back off. Immune to threats or punishments, this endangered species has one cardinal virtue in the game above all – doggedness.

Nicolas
Anelka

WHAT'S THE PROBLEM?

Nicolas Anelka

"I don't care about other people's opinions. I know what I want, that's all I care about."

Nicolas Anelka's career is really just a long string of bids for freedom, guided totally by his own instincts and not making total sense. He was undeniably gifted when, at 16 years of age, launched by former bad boy Luis Fernandez, he made his debut in the top flight of French football with Paris St Germain. He then converted to Islam, embracing a religion followed by many young men from the West Indies. Several months later, he became the first French player to sign for a foreign club, Arsenal, while still a minor. His first season in London was mediocre. His manager Arsene Wenger, who brought him over, gave him an ultimatum. "Either pull your finger out or leave the club!" Nicolas pulled his finger out and became one of the best forwards in Europe, so good, in fact, that he was called up to Aime Jacquet's French squad shortly before the 1998 World Cup. Although one of the first choices among the 28 players selected by the coach, in the end he was one of the six who were overlooked. He left his team-mates in the middle of the night, and was on the Eurostar during the World Cup final won by France.

However, he was the hero the following year in a superb England–France friendly (won 2–0 by France with two goals by Anelka) and was part of Arsenal's league and cup double-winning team. Despite this, he was transferred to Real Madrid in June 1999, a deal in which the Gunners were paid the tidy sum of £20 million.

One month later, Anelka missed three training sessions. The player was immediately suspended and had his salary docked for 45 days. Never had Real Madrid come down on one of its players so heavily. Anelka was 21, and basically didn't agree with the tactical choices of his technical manager Vicente Del Bosque. He would, however, be in the Real team that triumphed 3–0 against Valencia in 2000 in the final of the Champions League. It was a decent year for Nico, although he wouldn't win much with France following the European Championship. He was still behaving on the pitch, and was a good friend who got on well with his team-mates.

Nevertheless, it was clear that he wouldn't last long at Madrid. By a stroke of luck, a rejuvenated Paris St Germain qualified for the Champions League and signed him. But Anelka came up against his old coach Luis Fernandez over the course of the season, a renewal of ties that couldn't fail to produce sparks.

Anelka took refuge in England, at Manchester City, where he stayed for two and a half seasons, until 2006, longer than he stayed at any other club. Meanwhile, on November 17, 2002, he snubbed a call-up to the French team, now under Jacques Santini. He couldn't come to terms with not being called up one month earlier when Djibril Cisse, Olivier Kapo and David Trezeguet were ruled out. The coach had opted instead for Sidney Govou, Thierry Henry, Steve Marlet and Daniel Moreira.

"The coach thought I should prove that I really wanted to wear the blue shirt," he explained. "Above all, he showed me that he didn't really want to pick me. His arguments were far from convincing. He said that he had picked players over me because he knew them better. But, when the last team was selected, there were injuries and he didn't pick me. He doesn't want me."

The French football federation suspended him for two matches. Six months later, Nico struck back in *Paris Match*: "I don't need the French team. If the coach kneels down in front of me and apologizes, then I'll give it some thought. In my head, I've already ruled out Euro 2004. I'll make my own way without the French team."

Consequently, Anelka was at neither the European Championship nor the 2006 World Cup. Called back up to the team by Raymond Domenech, Nico could reasonably hope to feature on the list of 23 for the World Cup in Germany. He didn't. His comment: "It's like Domenech called me up just to break me. Unfortunately for him, I scored [in a 3–2 win over against Costa Rica]. It's like he'd decided not to pick me from the very beginning. If it comes down to that, why make me come back? As usual, I'm not judged by my sporting ability." He added: "I won't watch the World Cup."

Now 26, Nicolas Anelka went on to be worshipped at Fenerbahce, in Turkey, his club for the winter of 2004–05. You'd think that would be that. But, in the summer of 2006, he arrived back in the Premier League for the third time in his career, this time with Bolton, a club with a growing reputation for relaunching the careers of the disinherited.

Anelka, is not not your typical, run-of-the-mill bad boy. He is very guarded about his private life, but engaging with those who succeed in gaining his trust, and he remains not very sociable with others. Although he looks the part when he goes out, he is never happier than when staying in, mixing on his decks or playing tennis. "I don't care about other people's opinions. I know what I want, that's all I care about." ■

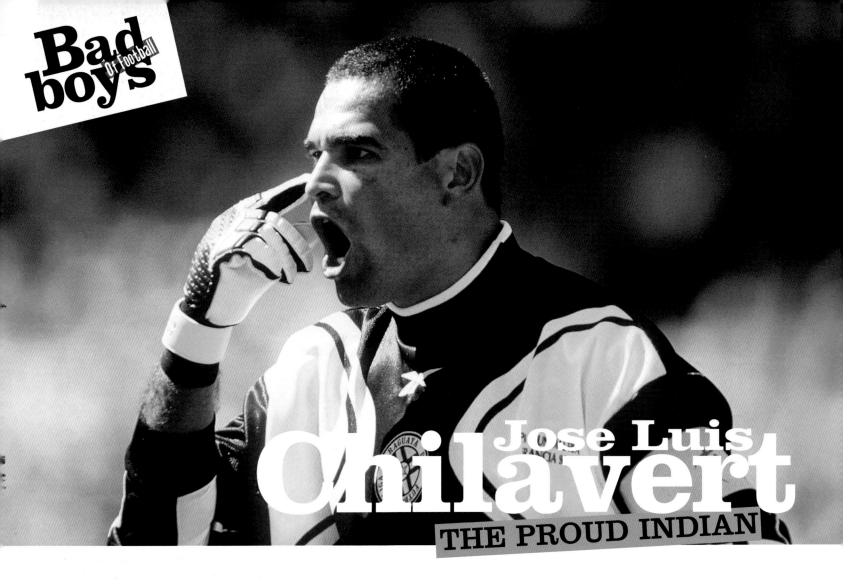

Jose Luis Chilavert

THE PROUD INDIAN

Jose Luis Chilavert takes great pride in both his appearance and his right hook. Six foot tall and weighing 14 stone, the former porter from Paraguay could have been a nightclub bouncer. Thanks to his strength, his iron will and the doggedness of his older brother, he came close to the very highest level of football.

He paraded his bad temper and aggressive nature on the pitches of Latin America and then France for nearly 25 years, without ever receiving the kind of punishment his temperament seemed to invite. His countless outbursts gave him a reputation he was very proud of, and which he summed up as follows: "I am a guarani Indian, I have my pride!"

His assaults included a kamikaze attack on Martin Palermo, centre-forward of Boca Juniors, the simulated strangulation of former Argentine play-maker Marcelo Gallardo, vicious punches handed out to a number of forwards and a kick up the backside of someone gathering the ball who was taking too long, in his view.

"I'm exposed in my position and I have to make sure they respect me", he said following a 2–0 defeat against Brazil during the qualifying rounds of the 2002 World Cup, having spat in the face of Brazilian defender Roberto Carlos, who'd poked fun at his Indian roots. As for

Chilavert making excuses, don't bet on it… "I'll never shake hands with a poof like Palermo. Argentinians think that Paraguayans should be working on building sites. They think we're Bolivians!" His comments on Maradona, Argentina's icon: "Chilavert is a bad guy. The last thing we need is for a bumpkin to explain to Argentinians how to play football."

That was hardly going to upset the Paraguayan goalkeeper, who could cope with paradox as easily as bad faith, and who responded: "Maradona is a drug addict and an alcoholic. He doesn't deserve to be part of the great family of football, because he sets such a bad example to youngsters."

The only real punishment handed down to Jose Luis Chilavert was by Argentina's legal system in 1996. Found guilty of beating the living daylights out of a storeman at Gimnisia y Esgrima la Plata, he was given a thirteen-month suspension and a three-month suspended prison sentence.

When not preoccupied with fostering his bad image, Chilavert devoted all his time to fostering a good one. On this quest, nothing was too fine or too expensive. The money he amassed as goalkeeper of San Lorenzo (his first professional club, in Argentina, from 1984 to 1988)

"Anything goes when you want to win. Winning means money!"

J. L. Chilavert

transformed his wardrobe into one that would have even Imelda Marcos, the extravagant wife of Philippine dictator Ferdinand Marcos, green with envy. During this period, he shaved his head every week, a trend followed by many in the mid-1990s. He used clippers to maintain his three-day stubble and his "just got out of bed" look. In Buenos Aires, he rented an apartment next to his own to house the multitude of jumpers, trousers, shirts and shoes he had purchased, as though turning his back on what should have been his fate. "As a kid, I sold the milk from our three scraggy cows. To hang on to the only pair of shoes I could have for the year, I played football with bare feet. In 1974, when I was nine, I watched the World Cup at the counter of the shop that had the only TV – it was black and white – in the neighbourhood."

Also making time for his ambitions during his younger years, Chilavert streaked up and down the waste grounds of his childhood playing centre-forward, the only position his ego allowed.

Unfortunately, to his humiliation, his older brother told him he couldn't be No. 9 as he wasn't tall enough to impose himself in a crowd of defenders. His brother also told him that his hands would give him the best chance of getting selected, and it was as goalkeeper that he made his debut for the small club of Sportivo Luqueno at the age of 15.

Ironically, this particular position was perfect, suiting his egocentric, bossy, but also generous nature. From the mid-1980s, he devoted himself with astonishing loyalty to the Paraguay national team, establishing himself as one of the best goalkeepers in the world for a number of years. With the Argentinian club Velez Sarsfield, which he took in hand with the help of coach Carlos Bianchi, formerly of Reims and Paris St Germain, he would win everything, or as good as: the Argentinian League title in 1992, the Copa Libertadores in 1994, the Intercontinental Cup, with a 2–0 victory over Fabio Capello's AC Milan the same year, the Copa Interamericana in 1995 and the SuperCopa in 1996. He was voted goalkeeper of the year by FIFA in 1995 and 1997 and best South American player in 1996.

During this prosperous period, however, his greatest achievement was, without doubt, Paraguay's qualification for the 1998 World Cup in France.

There, thanks to his charisma and influence on his team-mates, Paraguay came through the "group of death" along with Nigeria, while Spain and Bulgaria were knocked out.

In the second round of the knock-out stages, Chilavert was the reason all of France watched through their hands in a match that France won 1–0 thanks to a golden goal from Laurent Blanc in the 114th minute. French coach Aime Jacquet later admitted that he thought France were going out, as the penalty shoot-out would surely have gone against his men. "We came so close. I was expecting penalties," Chilavert confirmed. "I knew the crowd in Lens was worried. We missed our chance, but this match has shown Paraguay off to the whole world. Before, we didn't really exist."

Chilavert, with his acrobatic feats behind his defence, was never going to be content with the quiet role normally reserved for goalkeepers. He needed more, he wanted the same admiration given to players who hit the back of the net. He also moved up front on a regular basis. He scored a total of 62 goals over his professional career, eight of which were for his national team. The first was a penalty against his idol, Rene Higuita, during Paraguay's 2–1 win against Colombia in a qualifying match for the 1990 World Cup. Training always ended with a long free-kick practice session, with a line drawn only 6.5 metres away to increase the difficulty of the exercise.

Before ending his career at Velez in 2004 at the age of 39, Chilavert made a small detour through France and Racing Club Strasbourg, where he stayed for two seasons, from 2000 to 2002. Heavier (over 16 stone) and lacking motivation, the player never really established himself in Alsace, even though he gave Racing the French Cup in 2001 by scoring the decisive penalty in the final against Amiens (the game finished 0–0, and Racing won 5–4 on penalties), after saving another. Worse still, he was on bad terms with the club, which accused him of submitting a forged document to the authorities to support his demand for a compensation payment of €3.7 million (about £2.5 million). In 2005 he was given a six-month suspended sentence and ordered to pay €10,000 (just under £7,000) in damages. Not that this upset him much. "Anything goes when you want to win. Winning means money!" ∎

Luis Fernandez

THE WOUNDED MAN

He's engaging, and his story is touching. It's the tale of a kid brought up in Minguettes in the suburbs of Lyons, not afraid of rolling with the punches, having frequently been on the receiving end, who goes on to become the highest-paid footballer in France and the first French coach to win a European Cup. Not a bad way to change your destiny when you're born in Spain (Tarifa), lose your father at the age of six and then move to France.

Better at football than school, Luis Fernandez enjoyed himself at AS Minguettes. Untiring, resolute and not afraid to tackle, he plundered the pitches of the Lyons region. He was a good player and was scouted by several clubs, but was said to be too fiery, impetuous and quick-tempered. Hadn't he been suspended for six months with the Juniors for insulting a referee? After being given trials by Paris St Germain, he was finally accepted by the PSG training centre. Here he was taken in hand by Pierre Alonzo, his second dad, who was to train him, teach him and take him through to the first team. Luis forged his own character. Moving from one training session a week to two sessions a day was a shock, and being separated from his family was painful, but he coped with it. "Being on my own encouraged me to think like a winner. When I was 18, I was slapped in the face in the PSG dressing-room and I made sure that would never happen again. I'll never be the person who offers their cheek for a slap. That's the way I am, but I'm not a lout."

Fernandez knew that his game style could get him noticed. "On the pitch, it's my temperament and my strong character that stand out. You just couldn't understand how much I hate losing." Having obtained French citizenship, he joined the French national side in 1982, after the World Cup. He would stay in the team for ten years, winning 60 caps. Winner of the French Cup in 1982 and 1983 with PSG, he soon identified with the Paris club. He had the cheek and temperament of a "*titi*" (a "street urchin"), which he was proud of. "My style is quite aggressive, I've got a Latin temperament and that's what I play with. But I won't change. I'm not a snob and have a winner's mindset."

After Pierre Alonzo at the training centre, Francis Borelli, the president of PSG, was next to take him under his wing. In 1986 Luis Fernandez was French champion and part of the magic four (Fernandez, Tigana, Platini and Giresse) in the France team which won the 1984 European Championship and came third in the 1986 World Cup. >

Luis Fernandez

"The person who can scare me on the pitch has not been born!"

> ## "The world of football isn't one of finer feelings and innocent lambs. The perfect world, where coaches don't shout and groan on the bench, doesn't exist."

He took on the role of ugly duckling of this exceptional midfield, the one to pick up the cards and make the fouls, although deep down he suffered. "They've labelled me as a violent player, and that's very hard to accept. Some players get something out of winding me up, whereas I'm on the pitch to win. I go in for contact."

The sense of injustice consumed him, even when he signed for Matra Racing at the end of this incredible season. Seduced by the charisma of Jean-Luc Lagardere, as well as the salary he was offering (more than 500,000 francs, approx. £50,000, per month), he thought he'd be top dog of his new team, built on the back of millions. Wrong! Max Bossis was handed the reins of the team. There were arguments between the two men and with the directors. Luis Fernandez had been a traitor himself (to PSG) and now felt betrayed in turn, and the relationship broke down. Despite his amazing salary, Fernandez ended his third season at Racing with relegation to the second division.

He found sanctuary at Cannes and became the gang leader, the mouthpiece, finally, of the team. He began to notch up the cards. "The referees know me. They know I can't keep quiet when I think something's unfair. I've always been like that. I complain, I revolt, and then – bang! This accounts for probably 80 per cent of the cards I've received in my career. For the others, of course I've pulled a lot of shirts and shorts and accept the consequences. In any event, I've never hit anyone. It's simple, though. If you wind me up, I'll wind you up twice as much. The person who can scare me on the pitch has not been born!"

At Cannes, now aged 32, he shouted, groaned and buried his head in his shirt – all for real, of course. After a string of clashes, one of his knees gave way, requiring bone surgery, and it looked like the end of his career. But Fernandez gritted his teeth, hung in there and played again, and was exceptional! In the lead-up to the 1992 European Championship, he was even called up to the French squad by coach Michel Platini, who bestowed on him the ultimate honour, the No. 10 shirt. It was deserved, even if Fernandez was the leading recipient of red cards that season, with four sendings-off. At the championships, in Sweden, disillusionment set in. In Platini's mind, Luis was a big brother who could take the young lads in hand, a luxury substitute. Fernandez, on the other hand, had come to play. On the flight home, after losing to Denmark 2–1 in a match in which he only played one half, he vented his spleen, inelegantly, like a wounded man. He wouldn't be picked again.

Life was good at Cannes, however. Feeling his years creeping up on him, he became first player/coach and then just coach in December 1992. His gang leader mentality worked at Bocca. The crowds loved his windmill gestures and his systematic whistling to call a player back into line. Under Fernandez the club qualified twice for the European Cup in 1991 and 1994, and Fernandez the coach was now the darling of the French top flight.

To "give PSG something to smile about again", he was brought back to the Paris club at the end of the 1993–94 season. A close eye was kept on him right from the start, though, and he couldn't bear the fact that they didn't have complete confidence in him. Although PSG managed a grand slam in the Champions League (eight victories in a row in the preliminary round and group stages), relations between the club management and the fans' favourite soon became strained, only improving again in 1995 with a League Cup–French Cup double. In 1996, after winning the Cup Winners Cup, beating Rapid Vienna 1–0 in the final, a "bitter" Fernandez hot-footed it to Spain, to Atletico Bilbao, where he would remain until June 2000. He qualified the club for its first ever Champions League, but the Basque club's management board grew tired of his incessant twitching, his sometimes puzzling methods and his permanent state of over-excitement on the bench. During his second season, he was sent off and picked up a one-match suspension. Better still, on May 29, 1999, he was sent off the pitch and then found guilty of pushing the fourth official. He was suspended for six days. A record in the Spanish League, one he still held seven years later.

Luis Fernandez

When he returned to Paris in November 2000 following the dismissal of Philippe Bergeroo, he had the extensive powers of a general manager. The following season, however, his behaviour on the pitch got out of hand. On August 4, 2001, a first report on his behaviour in front of his dugout landed on the desk of the federation authorities. On August 11, he received a red card for dissent. He turned up very late for his hearing with the disciplinary committee, and received a two-match suspension. On September 15, another report. On November 29, 2001, he was again sent off during a PSG–Marseille match. This time, he picked up a one-match suspension and a fine of €3,800 (approx. £2,500). But even this didn't keep him quiet. His club was reeling, the fans were complaining, and the pressure was increasing. On March 2, 2002, during a League Cup match against Bordeaux, he was sent off again after being accused of shoving the fourth official.

His punishment was a six-month suspension. "The world of football isn't one of finer feelings and innocent lambs. The perfect world, where coaches don't shout and groan on the bench, doesn't exist," was all he said. He promised to mend his ways, but instead lost his way in a storm of poor results. Next, after piecework in Spain, at Espanyol Barcelone, which he saved from the drop, he hopped through various exotic lands (Al-Rayyan, in Qatar, and Beitar Jerusalem, in Israel, where there was an international arrest warrant out on club president Arcardi Gaydamak for arms trafficking) and radio studios, before returning as the saviour of Seville at the end of 2006 in an attempt to save Betis from relegation. In his *Luis Attaque* show on RMC Info, Fernandez had a whale of a time, tackling every which way and giving out good marks as well as red cards – which, he found, were much more fun to give than to receive. ∎

Gennaro
Gattuso
THE SCOTTISH RHINOCEROS

> ## "A perfect football match is one played on a winter night, in the rain, in the cold."

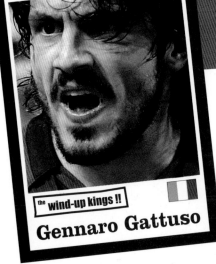

Gennaro Gattuso

There are two diametrically opposed sides to Gennaro Gattuso. On a day-to-day basis, we find a gentle, kind and rather cultured person. On the pitch, meanwhile, the lamb becomes a wolf, notable for harassment of his opponent, full-blooded tackles, intimidating looks and quasi-systematic contesting of referees' decisions. It would be wrong, however, to think that this was all there was to the talents of the AC Milan ball-winner, with his unbelievable physique and quirky, mad-professor beard. Gennaro Ivan Gattuso is, above all, an incredible scrapper with the ability to pull his team-mates along behind him.

"Technically, there are better players on this earth than Gattuso. But he has a heart that you can't beat, a pure soul. He's someone who'd never betray you. You'd go to the ends of the earth with Gattuso." These were the words of his coach, Carlo Ancelotti, who also played in defensive midfield alongside Franco Baresi, Frank Rijkaard and Marco Van Basten. "Provocation is part of the game, and if it happens a lot, I know it's because I'm a nuisance to my opponent," said Gattuso. "It doesn't bother me that my team-mates are better known than I am. I do my job, and I don't do it badly if the enquiries from other clubs are anything to go by."

This notion of sacrifice, struggle for the love of the shirt, seemed to become ingrained in the Italian. "For me, a perfect football match is one played on a winter night, in the rain, in the cold. It's so great to see the steam from the players' breath! When I play in conditions like this, which was so often what it was like in Scotland, it gives me even more of a boost."

It is no accident that he refers to Scotland. It was there that the legend began. After playing ten matches with Perugia, Gattuso signed for Glasgow Rangers in 1997, when he was only 19, on a free transfer made possible by the Bosman rule. The Rangers fans were expecting their Italian signing to be an elegant, creative player. Instead they saw a fighting spirit, an expert in kick and rush. "They thought they'd see an Italian, a technical player. What they found was a man more Scottish than they were. My style of play is more English than Italian. I'm strong, I run for ninety minutes, but there are loads of players one hundred per cent more technical than I am. My role is to run and win balls back. I'm not sad about it, I've always dreamed of playing how I play. I had a poster of Salvatore Bagni [the midfield ball-winner at Naples, then at Inter, in the 1980s] in my room, but not Michel Platini. In Scotland, it all clicked during a match against Celtic. I played an explosive game, in typical Gattuso style! Afterwards, I signed autographs!"

Nicknamed "the Rhinoceros" because of his angry charges, he played forty league games with Rangers. Noticed by Salernitana, Gattuso returned to Italy, before joining the great AC Milan the following season. But the Scottish chapter of his life had a profound effect on him, like an initiation. It was where he met Monica, his wife, and where he discovered himself. "There was so often excitement for me in Scotland. A man with heart, who plays with his heart, needs to hear his heart so he doesn't lose his way. In Glasgow, my heart really beat. People who haven't played football up there wouldn't understand. >

"I've got nothing to hide. All my doping test will show is pepper and sweat."

"There were so many things that stood out, particularly the young lads at the club who had to clean the boots of the first-team players. Sometimes I was in the dressing-rooms for eight hours a day. It was good. It was a really important part of my career. I had a lot of responsibilities at this great club, and it helped me to grow as a player and a person. I remember eating fish and chips before the derby against Celtic."

Bastion of AC Milan since 1999, Gattuso has now acquired another nickname, the "Bull of San Siro", and won titles: the Champions League in 2003 and 2007, the Italian Cup in 2003 and the Italian League title in 2004. He attributed his success largely to the strength of his family ties, notably his daughter Gabriela. "This little kid has changed my life. I don't know why I waited so long to have a kid. I can't wait until she's older and understands, for her to be proud of me – not of the footballer, of her father. Ever since she was born, I've tried to be a better person, in life and on the pitch. I'm sure that Monica and I will have another child. I hope we'll have a son. I want a son and heir."

It was a firm belief of the Gattuso family that the will is passed down from father to son. "I get my combativeness from my dad," said the son of Franco and Costanza, "and I get my humanity from my mum. They were brilliant. They taught me to how to behave in life and stopped me from making so many mistakes. As a kid, I remember I wanted to play truant, and went hitching. A car stopped. Disaster! It was my dad. He was furious. He took me straight to school and gave me a smacking in front of all my class-mates. It was the only punishment he gave me, and I learned my lesson. Dad always told me to be an honest man and advised me never to contest a referee's decision, even if it wasn't fair. But I admit that I forget this advice only too often, unfortunately."

Gattuso has also sometimes forgotten to attend drug tests. In March 2005, he was picked at random at the end of AC Milan's Serie A match against Rome, along with his team-mate Giuseppe Pancaro. The two Rossoneri ("the Red and Blacks") took the urine test, but were said to have refused the blood test to detect EPO use. "We didn't refuse," protests Gattuso, "but, when we came in, there was total chaos in the room. I asked if the test was compulsory and was told it wasn't, so I left a larger amount of urine, as provided for in the regulations."

He then added: "I've got nothing to hide. All my doping test will

show is pepper and sweat." In any event, this ball-winner, with his compact physique (5'8" tall and weighing around 12 stone), continued to impose himself in the rough Sunday scraps in the Calcio. Happy, glowing, almost calm, the fighter with the red and black blood had only one fear left: "That the fire in me eventually goes out!"

Although Gattuso won a World Cup winner's medal in 2006, he didn't get ideas above his station, and this, without doubt, is what made him so popular in Italy. Gattuso's crazy and jovial nature is expressed in his own unique style, as demonstrated in this extract of an interview with coach Marcello Lippi, when asked about his eventual departure just after their final victory over France:

Interviewer: "Gattuso said that he threatened you with the words: 'If you leave, I'll kill you …'"

Lippi: "I never heard him say that. He did give me a couple of slaps, though. That was his way of celebrating major events. The last time, he pretended to strangle me."

Gattuso is outgoing, but modest with it, as he showed when a journalist compared his importance on the pitch to that of Ronaldinho. The Italian famously replied: "That's an insult to football. I work hard. He has class!" ■

Oliver Kahn

THE SQUARE JAW

"In this business, only winning and money count. The past counts for nothing and that's fine with me. The day that doesn't apply any more, they'll be only too quick to turf you out the window."

the wind-up kings !!

Oliver Kahn

At six foot and weighing around 15 stone, Oliver Kahn has an extraordinary kind of density, as though this imposing mass of a man, with his fixed and searing gaze, has grown with each of the many knocks in his life and on the pitch. At Karlsruhe, where he started his footballing career as sweeper, at first they didn't want him on the field. He drew back into goal, without a word. From then, each of his successes was a hard-fought, long-running battle.

He was 18 when he became a full team member in the Bundesliga, but he conceded four goals in one match, followed by two more in next one. Then zero, because he was left on the bench. He had to wait another two seasons before he managed to break through in 1990, but after that he did not leave his post until July 1994, the month he left for Bayern Munich. For the person who had hero-worshipped Sepp Maier, No. 1 of the 1974 German World Cup-winning team, who became goalkeeping coach of Bayern, this was the realization of a dream and all his hard work. "He's work mad," his team-mates said of him. Olli retorted: "Fierce determination and pride have got me where I am today. Work too."

Even after serious injury, he continued to make a strong impression on his colleagues, bawling at them like a madman when he thought it necessary, and on opposing strikers when he rushed ferociously out of his area. Prepared to leave an imprint of his studs on an opponent's shin or an elbow in his back, it never kept him from a good night's sleep. "I take risks too. So yes, I've an aggressive style of play, but in the good sense of the word. For me, being aggressive means being there one hundred per cent. I never want to have to criticize myself for not having given everything during a match. That said, I'm not the same when I leave the field."

Off the pitch, he was known as a friendly person who liked to dabble in the stock market occasionally. He was also unfaithful, on occasion, to Simone, his childhood sweetheart whom he would later go on to marry. On one such occasion, he was snapped in compromising company, a glass of beer in one hand and a BMW customer service adviser in the other.

Hugely impressed, in his teenage years, by the book *Jonathan Livingston Seagull*, by Richard Bach, a parable on the desire to constantly excel, Kahn never gave in – not when he was the whipping boy of the opposing fans, and was hit on the head by conkers, in 1994, and a golf ball, in 1999; not when a vigorous dispute with Andreas Herzog of Werder Bremen made the front page of all the German papers, in 1996; not even when he knocked out one of his own team-mates, defender Samuel Kuffour, just before a Champions League match in Glasgow in 1999.

In April 2005, he made no bones about laying into Willy Sagnol after Bayern were knocked out by Chelsea in the quarter-finals of the Champions League. "Willy lacked desire and determination against Joe Cole. He should have stopped him from crossing. Not even a veteran would have been that static." The criticism was characteristically outspoken, but the dry response of the French international delighted the German tabloid press: "If I had to recall all of Kahn's errors this season, I'd need at least ten minutes." The next time they played, the two team-mates were to be seen arm in arm.

Looking back at a career that had some definite low points, like having to wait five years after his first national team call-up in 1995, having spent the 1994 World Cup on the bench, before he was made the number-one goalkeeper behind a team of oldies during the German disaster that was Euro 2000, Kahn confessed: "I always thought that one day I'd reach the top, but there was a lot of naivety in that." Nothing was given to him on a plate, and he took all he could without asking. Sepp Maier underlined the willpower of a player with talent (but not all that much), who had to bide his time to get what he wanted: "Kahn had it all because he always wanted to have it all. I've never seen anyone get stuck in like he does" – which Oliver interprets as: "If you've never had it tough, you'll never get anywhere." >

"Being number two, I couldn't even imagine it!"

in 1994 and 1998, he would have to go back to the hotel and rip up cushions to release the anger he felt at being left on the bench. Talking of this episode in the life of the bad boy, Oliver has described it as "an ordeal" and spoken of "terrible frustration", "real sadness" and "a time to grow and discover myself".

"It was hard, very hard. I had to accept that I was no longer the number one after two seasons in which I won the Cup and the league title with Bayern and during which I never stopped thinking about the World Cup. You can't imagine what that feels like. It's a blow, a big blow. I'm not unbreakable any more, I'm sensitive." One suspected it, but Oliver had to wait until he was 37, and probably his last World Cup finals, to realize it.

During the competition, he showed total support for the new number one, encouraging him and even giving him a massage before the penalty shoot-out in the quarter-finals against Argentina (which Germany won 4–2 after the game finished 1–1). This was the price of Germany's successful progression through the World Cup, and Olli had to grit his teeth and accept being sickeningly cast against type … as a good guy. ∎

In return, Kahn found that he wouldn't have to be bothered with trifling matters of discipline. In the national team and at his club, he was his own boss. In the winter of 2005, he missed training at Bayern to shoot advertisements in Japan, where they were crazy about his fair hair and square jaw.

He had no doubt, however, that Jurgen Klinsmann would choose him as the number-one keeper for the World Cup hosted by Germany. "Being number two, I couldn't even imagine it!" he declared. In May 2006, however, he faced the truth: he would be on the bench. Just as

Bad boys Of Football

Jens Lehmann

THE PENALTY-AREA MOANER

"I've nothing to be ashamed of."

Poor Jens has spent almost his whole career in the looming shadow of his main competitor in the German team, Oliver Kahn. But Jens Lehmann had the last word. Just before the 2006 World Cup, coach Jurgen Klinsmann recognized his loud-mouth qualities and made him number one, much to Kahn's disgust. What made the decision all the braver was that Germany's first match was to be at Munich, Kahn's stronghold.

This 6 foot-plus German did not look the part – he looked more like a string bean. Before signing for the Gunners in 2003, there were various clues pointing to the fact that this guy was not like everyone else. Born in Essen, he remains deeply attached to the Ruhr, Germany's industrial heartland where the motorways are lined with factories, and goes back there whenever he can.

At the beginning of his professional career, with Schalke 04, he was taken off during a 6–1 defeat by Leverkusen. He was so upset that he left the stadium and returned home on public transport, a small trip of some 50 kilometres, which gave him just about enough time to calm down. He was also the first goalkeeper in the Bundesliga to score a goal in normal play, equalizing for Schalke at the end of a 2–2 draw with Dortmund. The following summer, he transferred to AC Milan, but it was a mistake. He failed to fit in and sat on the bench alone, taciturn and silent. In 1998, after half a season and just five matches with the Rossoneri, he surprised everyone by signing for Borussia Dortmund, Schalke's sworn enemy. Early on, however, he made the mistake of pledging his eternal devotion to his old club, thereby turning the local

Jens Lehmann

fans against him right from the start. Lehmann was also sent off after crossing the pitch to bawl out one of his own team-mates, Brazilian player Marcio Amoroso, for not making enough effort in defence.

Like Eric Cantona, he likes to paint, but refuses to show his work to anyone. He has studied economics, worn Nike gloves for internationals even though the German team was equipped by Adidas, declared that the Adidas ball provided for the World Cup was "a plastic shell", and dared to deliberately shove Bastian Schweinsteiger into the advertising hoardings of the ArenA during the inaugural match between Bayern and the German national team – clearly not bothered about being booed by the Bavarian crowds. The bad boy with the mop of curly hair even wound up the follically challenged Carsten Jancker to the point where they came to blows.

In 2003, he moved to Arsenal where, despite his mediocre performances at the start, he never admitted any failing. "I've got nothing to be ashamed of," said Jens. As his reputation had preceded him, it did not take the English press long to give him the nickname "Jens the nutter". Under the firm hand of Arsene Wenger, however, the tormented soul calmed down. He improved, matured and became more consistent. For Jens, life in London was relaxed, both on and off the pitch. In the last minute of the semi-final of the Champions League against Villareal on April 25, 2006, he stopped Riquelme's penalty, earning his team qualification with a 1–0 aggregate victory, and was given a new nickname: "Superman".

In the final against Barcelona, however, his temperament proved to be fatal to his club. In the 19th minute, he came out of his area to meet the onrushing Samuel Eto'o and, with a cool pair of gloves, brought the player down. Not unreasonably, he was sent off. This was the first time a red card had been shown during a Champions League final. Arsenal never recovered and finally lost 2–1.

During the 2006 World Cup, Jens became a national hero when he stopped the penalties of the Argentines Ayala and Cambiasso in the quarter-finals (Germany winning 4–2 on penalties after the game finished 1–1). But he refused to be carried around triumphantly by his team-mates, preferring instead to return quickly to the dressing-room, as if to show, once again, how different he was, and how indifferent to the feelings of the public. ∎

Ahmed Hossam, aka
"Mido"
MR PIGHEADED

the wind-up kings !!

Mido

One could call Mido "the Egyptian Nicolas Anelka". With his escapades, rows with his coaches and constant changes of club, he bears comparison. The story of Ahmed Hossam, known as "Mido", began in a residential neighbourhood of Cairo. From a middle-class background, he started out at Zamalek, the main local club of which his dad was a supporter. It didn't take Mido long to decide that if his career was going to develop he needed to go to Europe. Spotted by PSG, he spent a number of months in the Paris club's training centre before leaving.

Through a Belgian agent, the striker with the velvet left foot moved to La Gantoise, even though Zamalek had confiscated his passport. Mido shone in Belgium, scored goals but showed a stubborn streak. "He's a nice guy, but he's temperamental, unpredictable and selfish. He's pigheaded and it's like he lives in a bubble," was how his old team-mate Jerome Lempereur summed him up. The marriage with La Gantoise ended with a gloves-off divorce. **>**

> ## "The coach is an amateur. The people at the Federation are amateurs. They think they know everything, but the truth is they know nothing."

Next, a new chapter at Ajax Amsterdam: a brilliant start followed by nights out, set-tos with his coach and finally his departure a year later. It was like groundhog day each season. Mido played at Celta Vigo for one year, then Olympique Marseille (2003–04), then AS Rome and finally Tottenham. He stayed in London for a year and a half, topping his loyalty record, but Tottenham let him go for the 2006–07 season.

It was his coaches who summed up pigheaded Mido the best. "As a coach, you have to make sure Mido doesn't make a fool of you," explained Frenchman Patrick Remy, who managed Mido at La Gantoise. "He is totally unprofessional and thinks he's a star," was the verdict of Ronald Koeman, his boss at Ajax. "Even if I had to play with ten men, I wouldn't have him back." Leo Beenhakker, technical director of the legendary Amsterdam club, concurred: "Every coach comes up against one unmanageable player in their career. For me, it was Mido!"

Alain Perrin, his first coach at Olympique Marseille, was rather milder: "He needs to learn about the requirements of a professional club and conform to the club rules." Jose Anigo, who also managed him at OM, had the same view of him: "He's a good lad, but he needs to understand that even if he has loads of potential, sometimes the collective rule is law. You can't just put up with anything." The grievances of his coaches included his nights out, his tendency to over-eat, his repeated late arrivals for training, a total lack of self-awareness, his regrettable habit of inventing injury when he was told he was not going to start and, finally, his readiness to leave the stadium when substituted during a match.

Mido's relations with the Egypt national team were even more ambiguous. He adored his country and proudly wore the prestigious Egypt shirt. At the same time, he seemed incapable of respecting the coach's rules. Often absent from meetings, he first of all attracted the wrath of Marco Tardelli. When the Italian was fired, the situation worsened with his successor Hassan Shehata. During the 2006 African Cup of Nations, which Egypt hosted, the coach decided to replace him during a match, a decision supported by the 74,000-strong crowd who, having watched his poor performance in this

semi-final against Senegal, cried "Off!" Furious, the Tottenham attacker refused to leave the pitch and violently berated his coach for a good few minutes.

Exasperated, his team-mates condemned the player's umpteenth outburst. First humiliation: they'd finally had it with him, which was just the first of several humiliations. Second, Zaki, his replacement, scored the winning goal in Egypt's 2–1 victory. Third, Egypt won the competition three days later, without his help. Fourth, the firm hand of the Egypt coach was largely praised throughout the country, as demonstrated by the huge ovation from the stands when Hassan Shehata climbed the podium. The magnanimous coach nevertheless allowed Mido to return to the group and collect his medal. He didn't, however, feature on the match sheet.

Faced with all these criticisms, Mido had two possible strategies. Counter-attack or withdraw. "Ronald Koeman has a strange mentality. He doesn't like the fact that others come before him. He's given me a bad image," he explained. Speaking about Shehata, Mido was no less offensive: "To be honest, I think he's a joke, really. He's a small-timer. Before he was the Egypt coach, he was coaching a team in the second division. I didn't even know him and I don't need to speak to him. The coach is an amateur. The people at the Federation are amateurs. They think they know everything, but the truth is they know nothing."

At times, however, he has tried to take the honourable route and make amends. "I apologize for my mistakes. I've no right to decide when I play or don't play in the national side," the striker said in February 2005, before continuing, "I know that I've sometimes been uncompromising in my dealings with the press, but I'm more experienced now. I also know that even the best players like Beckham or Zidane have had rows with the press. I now accept that I can be criticized, and that I shouldn't over-react when it happens." There was just one problem: by wasting his energy on pointless rows and changing his club as others change clothes Mido lost his way as a player. At the end of 2007 Mido's tally of trophies was just one, the Dutch Supercup. ∎

UMBRO

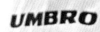

Fair Play

Stuart
Pearce
« PSYCHO »

the **wind-up kings !!**

Stuart Pearce

"It was a myth that worked in my favour, so I didn't stamp on it. People said I was hot-headed."

Englishman Stuart Pearce epitomizes footballers of old: consistent, tireless, one hundred per cent enthusiastic, prepared to move mountains for his love of the shirt. In short, a proper "made in England" player, a hard-working left-back, thankless position though it may be.

He started at Wealdstone FC, where he played part-time, working as an electrician the rest of the day. With his modest background, he didn't have a choice … In 1983, he was signed by Coventry City and then transferred two years later to Nottingham Forest. Pearce spent twelve seasons there, winning the League Cup on two occasions and losing a Cup final.

Following Nottingham Forest's relegation, he left the club for Newcastle, but always remained a favourite in the hearts of the Forest fans, who had affectionately given him the nickname "Psycho" – the nutter. Pearce, a clever left-sided defender, in fact gave his all on the pitch. Passionate? Definitely. Committed? Undeniably. Violent? Doubtful. Nevertheless Stuart was saddled for a long time with this reputation as a tough guy, an unrepentant tackler prepared to scythe down the opposing winger. "It was a myth that worked in my favour, so I didn't stamp on it. People said I was hot-headed, but I've played thousands of matches over my career and was only sent off five times."

This "misunderstanding" undoubtedly stemmed from his demeanour on the pitch, the unfailing motivation written all over his face, or the way he hoofed free-kicks. It also, however, stemmed from one or two outbursts, like when he insulted a referee. "I only did that once," said Pearce for the record. "Aggression was part of my game, but I learned to keep my self-control if I thought my behaviour could threaten team spirit or the result of the match. It's common sense." >

> **"Aggression was part of my game,** but I learned to keep my self-control if I thought my behaviour could threaten team spirit or the result of the match. **It's common sense."**

This reputation was also linked to one or two small errors of youth, silly misdeeds during his teenage years or even his well-known love of punk music (Pearce has seen the Stranglers in concert about 30 times). His autobiography, simply called *Psycho*, which came out in 2001, reveals a simpler yet more complex character, whose life was far from the stereotypical one of football, beer, birds, nights out and rock and roll.

Pearce, who became manager of Manchester City, has in fact spent twenty years, half of his life, with the same girl, Liz. He also lives a quiet life and is not in the least bit vain, to the extent that he would sometimes have to force himself to change out of his tracksuit after training sessions. Above all, he upholds such old-fashioned values as "respecting others", "detesting insolence" and accepting defeat without laying the blame on the referee.

It also seemed as if the passing of time had calmed him down. His receptiveness to journalists, his mild manner and his level-headedness all seemed out of keeping with his reputation as a cantankerous player. The young manager was also notable for his sense of fair play. In October 2005, when Thierry Henry and Robert Pires failed to score with their extraordinary double act from the penalty spot during a match against Arsenal, which City lost 1–0, Stuart said: "The referee made his decision in total honesty. If Pires and Henry had pulled it off, everyone would have thought it was an excellent idea. What's wrong with trying something new in football?"

Stuart Pearce is also known as a man of his word, and has an astonishingly indifferent relationship with money. He trained Manchester City for a year without even having a contract – strange behaviour in today's money-driven game – although he did straighten his situation out in March 2006. "I've had luck to earn a good living as a footballer and now as a manager. I'm not going to split hairs for a few quid more or less on my contract. My wife thinks I'm an idiot, but that's the way I see things."

A methodology that seems to work for the former left-back who won 78 England caps. Liked by his players because he's a good teacher and listener, Pearce stabilized City in the Premiership table, until they dismissed him in May 2007. The FA even considered him for the England manager's position after the departure of Sven-Goran Eriksson at the end of the 2006 World Cup in Germany. Keen? Pearce called it the "best job in the world". In the end it was Steve McClaren who was chosen, but it's undoubtedly only a matter of time for this young 44-year-old manager and former assistant of Kevin Keegan. Awarded an MBE, he's embarked upon his new path with a clear air of success. Now "cool", he imparts to others his raging desire to win without getting worked up and gets his point across without raising his voice. Not so mad, this "Psycho"! ■

"I risked my life to stop Fazekas."

Pfaff
Jean-Marie

the **wind-up kings !!**

Jean-Marie Pfaff

THE DESPERADO

As much through pride in his humble origins as his argumentative nature, Jean-Marie Pfaff used to take pleasure, when asked about his background, in revealing what his parents did for a living. They used to sell carpets door to door, accompanied by some of young Jean-Marie's eight brothers and sisters.

As a teenager, curly-haired as a sheep, strong as a ram and stubborn as a goat, he quickly became the star player of SK Beveren, where he had been in goal since the age of six. Carried away by his own exploits, he developed a spectacular and risky style of play. Playing for Belgium for the first time in 1976, in a match won 2–1 by Holland, he saved a penalty. Winner of the Belgian Cup in 1978 and then the league title with Beveren the following year, he became both a liability and an indispensable player. His pranks wound people up and he was dropped from the national team. He later returned to play in Euro 80 in Italy, where Belgium reached the final of the competition, losing 2–1 to West Germany. The following year, he was suspended for three months after kneeing a linesman on the way back to the dressing-room after a Cup tie against Lokeren. "I have a clear conscience," was all he had to say in his defence.

In 1982, during the World Cup in Spain, he set tongues wagging by staging a pretend drowning in the hotel swimming pool, throwing the entire Belgian delegation into a state of alarm. It was a stupid prank involving a journalist who'd offered to teach him to swim, according to Pfaff. He was outspoken in criticizing the manager's selections and the quality of some of his team-mates, particularly the defenders. At times he instilled fear, as when he came off his line to meet the Hungarian Laszlo Fazekas, who had burst into flight during

the first round of the World Cup. "I risked my life to stop Fazekas," boasted Pfaff, over the moon about saving his team's skin and earning a 1–1 draw.

In 1982, he joined Bayern Munich where another legendary, steely-eyed goalkeeper, the great Sepp Maier, took him under his wing as his spiritual son. At Bayern, "FC Hollywood", where he stayed for good, rows between players were tolerated, even encouraged, as long as they got the club talked about and performance on the pitch remained at a high level. This applied to Pfaff, who was three times German champion (1985, 1986 and 1987).

He was at the top of his game, and frequently alone against the world… During a 1986 World Cup qualifying match in Albania, he didn't trust the local food and brought his own. All the players fell ill, except him! Belgium lost 2–0 and had to face the play-off stages to reach the final phase in Mexico. Why hadn't he shared his concerns? "They wouldn't have believed me." As for his team-mates, they were, in his view, either too slow, not used to their best advantage or unable to execute a technical piece of play. "If I were Guy Thys [the coach], I would have sent one or two lads home from the World Cup. I played with a foot injury because the number two injured his shoulder playing tennis. No sooner does he get his act together, the wheels come off with that bloke!"

It was partly thanks to another of his risky sorties off his line that Belgium lost their 1986 World Cup semi-final 2–0 to Maradona's Argentina, but it was Jean-Marie Pfaff who was celebrated in the Grand'Place when the Red Devils returned to Brussels. Still popular ten years after his retirement from the game, followed by cameras wherever he went, he would later be the star of one of Belgium's first reality TV programmes. But, without his sense of anticipation and legendary temerity, Jean-Marie lost his groove. He turned everyone against him in 1999 when coaching at Ostende: he lost a players' vote by 18 votes to 0. Everyone admired his enthusiasm, but he was judged to be lacking not only in organizational skills but also in both theoretical and tactical knowledge. Pfaff, however, has not given up his ambition of one day becoming the Belgian squad's goalkeeping coach. ■

Fabrizio Ravanelli
BEWARE OF THE BUFFALO!

"Ravanelli is the bad boy that we need at Marseille. He suits the club and city's rebellious image. We don't have, and we never have had, a squeaky clean image here."

JEAN-MICHEL ROUSSIER

Driving force on the pitch, intelligent bulldozer, rebellious buffalo, diver, actor, unrepentant moaner, and a scorer too. Fabrizio Ravanelli was all of these. He was born in Perugia in the heart of Italy in 1968, although there was only ever one club for him: Turin's Juventus. At the age of seven, when he played at the local club, he saw Perugia defeat the Juve 1–0 on the last day of the League season. The home crowd went mad at the victory, but Fabrizio cried – his favourites had lost the title. From that point on, he only had one goal, to play with Juve. His path to achieving that goal, however, was a tortuous one.

After turning pro in Serie B, he made a name for himself at Perugia (41 goals in 90 matches), but didn't settle at Avellino. Transferred, he perked up again at Casertana (12 goals in 27 matches) and then at Reggina (24 goals in 66 matches). When he joined Juventus in 1992, he was already 23, had never previously played in Serie A and was only the fifth-ranked forward, behind Gianluca Vialli, Roberto Baggio, Pierluigi Casiraghi and Paolo Di Canio. At the end of his first match, Juventus boss Giovanni Agnelli told his coach, Giovanni Trapattoni: "I think this guy Ravanelli is laughable. It's the first time in Juve's history that we've had a laughable player!" Despite this, the "Trap" stood firm, as did Marcello Lippi, his successor, who incorporated "Penna Bianca" ("White Feather", on account of his prematurely white hair), into his famous attacking trio (Ravanelli, Vialli, Baggio) in front of Alessandro Del Piero. The unit worked fantastically. Juventus won the Cup and League double in 1995 and the Champions League in 1996, Ravanelli scoring their only goal in the final, which finished 1–1 (Juve winning 4–2 on penalties). Ravanelli scored a total of 41 goals in Serie A and, remarkably, all five goals in the club's 5–1 thrashing of CSKA Sofia in a 1994 UEFA Cup match.

He had achieved his goal. He was earning billions of lira, wearing shades and two-tone shoes and acting the star, but this didn't go down well with Juve, and Lippi in particular, who couldn't tolerate the pig-headed nature of his "Buffalo" any longer. In 1996, he placed him on the transfer list. Years later, Ravanelli still felt the humiliation. "Juve didn't respect me. I was deeply hurt." In a fit of pique, Ravanelli signed for Middlesbrough in England, which was to drop down to the Second Division with him. He scored 16 goals in the Premier League, but proved unforgiving towards his team-mates. "They're mad in England! You see lads who don't train during the week, and turn up on Saturday and their game's all over the place."

the **wind-up kings !!**
Fabrizio Ravanelli

He went to war with his managers. "I didn't want to play in the Second Division and they didn't want to let me go." This conflict would prevent Ravanelli from playing for nearly six months.

He finally moved to Olympique Marseille on a transfer deal worth just over £4 million and a monthly salary of nearly £90,000 before tax. "Ravanelli is the bad boy we need at Marseille," said the club president, Jean-Michel Roussier. "He suits the club and city's rebellious image. We don't have, and we never have had, a squeaky clean image here." Although he cut the perfect image climbing from his car in the Velodrome car park, Fabrizio struggled to establish himself on the pitch. Out of form, he often found himself chasing the game to no avail. Except on November 9, 1997 in the Parc des Princes. That day he performed a technically perfect dive to win a penalty and a 2–1 victory for his team. This caused a scandal in the puritan world of French football. Ravanelli was booed and whistled all over the country, to the point where his coach, Rolland Courbis, who had brought the player in, doubted whether he could keep him. "If Fabrizio can't play without being booed, a parting of ways seems unavoidable. It's not even a sporting issue that we have to resolve any more, it's a financial and business issue. Marseille doesn't want to complicate things for itself when things are already complicated enough. We hired him to be a plus, but he's become a minus … The press has labelled him a cheat, a thief, and look at the result!"

People in the business were surprised that someone of Ravanelli's metal could not overcome this temporary aggravation. However, the referees' body, which was now keeping a close eye on him, complained: "Mr Ravanelli constantly contests refereeing decisions. It's never his fault, he's always raising his arms to the heavens or burying his head in his hands."

In any event, he was offered to AC Milan in 1998, then Juve in 1999, and was turned down. Further humiliation, and his career was on a downward path … ■

"Life isn't always easy in Croxteth…"

ROONEY

8

Wayne Rooney
THE STREET PLAYER

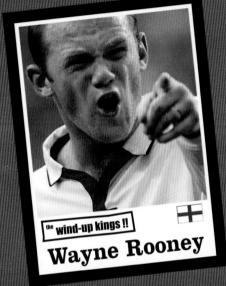

the wind-up kings !!
Wayne Rooney

A rumour began to go around. There was a 15-year-old called Wayne Rooney, doing amazing things in the Everton youth teams, but his future was uncertain. The lad was said to be unstable and dangerous, with a strong propensity for smacking anything that moved and a tendency to raise his elbows. There were numerous reports, and they added up. Fans confirmed that they'd seen Rooney in the pubs, drunk and out of control. Some added that they'd paid his taxi fare home so he could avoid a hammering from his bosses. People were worried, and expected the worst. Now a prophecy began to go around. Wayne Rooney, the most gifted player in England, would be dead at 20: shoulders not broad enough, lacking the necessary support around him …

Wayne Rooney was born in Croxteth, an area in the east of Liverpool that was troubled by unemployment, everyday violence, teenage pregnancies. His father, suffering with recurrent back pain, had to retire early from his job as a packer. He drew a small invalidity pension and spent his days in front of the box. His mother, Jeanette, was a canteen lady and earned around £130 a week – financial poverty, intellectual poverty. On the streets of Croxteth, Wayne Rooney had to fight for respect, leading him very early on to sign up at a boxing gym, where he cultivated his wind-up capabilities. "Life isn't always easy in Croxteth …" was all he said.

When the boy signed his first contract, the local mafia raised its head. Like Michael Owen before him, the Everton attacker was the victim of intimidation. Three large-calibre bullets were fired into agent Paul Stretford's door. The police intervened, and Everton hired bodyguards to protect its star. The story made the front page of the *News of the World*, then gradually died down. Later, at a birthday party for Colleen, Wayne's fiancee, his mum lost the plot. She chatted up the Everton players, climbed on tables and stirred up a mass brawl. The two families faced up to each other. The men agreed to settle the matter fairly, in the ring. This time, the story made the front page of the *Sun*. You can take the boy out of Croxteth, but you can't take Croxteth out of the boy … >

"It was a mistake you make when you're young."

His background moulded his behaviour on the pitch. Rooney ran straight and struck hard. His game was pure – limited, some said. Hugh Sleight, journalist at *Four Four Two*, remembers: "I was there at his first photo session for Nike, at the beginning of 2004. During the breaks, he had a ball to play around with. I've seen so many players in this kind of situation and, almost always, they perform tricks with the ball, passing it over their head, keeping it on the back of their neck etc. Not Rooney! He passed and struck the ball against a studio wall, hitting it harder and harder each time ..." David Moyes, his manager at Everton, used to say: "He's a street player." A dark Liverpool street, obviously, where the physical rules, and where clever tricks and fancy footwork are regarded as foreign nonsense.

Several weeks after making his debut as a professional (August 17, 2002, aged 16 years and 9 months), Rooney played in his first derby, against Liverpool. The lad tensed his muscles and lined up the tackles and physical challenges. Converging on a deep ball from the left, he clattered into Chris Kirkland, leaving the Reds goalkeeper dazed on the ground. Rooney jumped back up without a word or an excuse, and went back to join the fray. The unpleasant image was broadcast everywhere, and his reputation grew ... a fantastic bad boy.

Rooney was not vicious, but his desire got the better of reason. Altercations, hassling of referees, yellow cards by the bucket load, systematic suspensions. The striker regularly made the front page of the tabloids. Writers grabbed their pens, the same ones that wrote about Eric Cantona some years earlier. They shouted, raged, condemned, accused, and the presses turned ...

On February 12, 2003, Wayne Rooney won his first international cap against Australia and quickly established himself as the linchpin of the England team. Later, in Euro 2004 in Portugal, Rooney played four matches and scored four goals. After this, he joined Manchester United and continued to develop. Reined in tightly by manager Alex Ferguson, he behaved himself – most of the time ... One Sunday morning, England nearly choked on its bacon and eggs. The *News of the World* had published photos of Wayne Rooney in a Liverpool brothel. The tabloid explained, with all the gory details, that the star had signed autographs, paid for his sessions and speedily settled the matter in hand. Reading between the lines, it seemed that Rooney was a regular visitor. The striker kept a low profile for several days. "It was a mistake you make when you're young," he finally said. He wouldn't let himself be caught out again, promise!

His behaviour on pitch disintegrated, to the delight of the scandal press, reaching a peak during the 2006 World Cup. During the quarter-finals against Portugal, after being fouled by Ricardo Carvalho, he overtly stamped on the groin of the Portuguese defender. Cristiano Ronaldo, Rooney's team-mate at Manchester United, rushed up to the referee to demand a red card. Rooney's sending-off in the 62nd minute forced his team-mates to play with ten men for the rest of the second half and until the end of extra time, when there was still no score and England lost 3–1 on penalties. The *News of The World* ran the headline "Tears and a clown", while the *Mail on Sunday* went one better: "Ten men and a young idiot". In August 2006, when training began again at Manchester United, Ronaldo and Rooney's was rather a cool reunion. Soon, however, to the disappointment of the press, it was business as usual. ∎

Dennis Wise

THE BELLIGERENT TERRIER

"Wise could start a fight in an empty house."

SIR ALEX FERGUSON

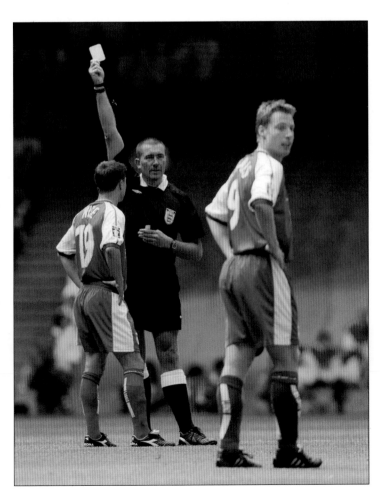

the **wind-up kings !!**

Dennis Wise

You can't love everyone, but sometimes it turns out no one loves you. The south London club, Millwall, made this into its motto: "No one likes us, we don't care!" Infamous for its hooligan problem, racist overtones and the unnerving atmosphere of its stadium, the Second Division team went a manager that would suit it. Dennis Wise was that man.

When he started at Millwall at the end of the summer of 2002, the former Chelsea hero had a long and troubled past behind him. The English international played eleven seasons with the Blues (1990–2001) before joining Leicester, only to be fired a year and a half later for hitting one of his team-mates. "Wise could start a fight in an empty house," was Sir Alex Ferguson's caustic observation on this cantankerous and tireless Dennis as a young player. This is a fairly good summary of his temperament. "Anything goes when winning's involved," Wise once said. "I grew up on a council estate in Shepherd's Bush," he also said. "It's a rough area and you had to know how to cope, but I just seemed to constantly attract trouble." >

> "I grew up on a council estate in Shepherd's Bush. **It's a rough area and you had to know how to cope,** but I just seemed to constantly attract trouble."

For Wise, football was a way of avoiding ending up as a small-time criminal hanging out on street corners. He supported Queen's Park Rangers, his local team, at the time. His salvation came in the form of an offer from Southampton, who took Wise on as an apprentice in 1981. "At 14 or 15, I wasn't doing too badly, but this was a chance for me to pull myself up. Things would have turned out badly for me if I hadn't," he admitted.

But even the discipline taught at football training centres has its limits, and there are some characters who will simply resist it. Wise managed to get expelled from a pre-selection trial for the English youth team after ransacking a train with a few of his team-mates. Not in the mood to compromise, he shut the door on Southampton and returned to London in 1985.

He was just 18 when he signed his first professional contract with Wimbledon, which had just moved up to the Second Division. Here he found a group of pranksters who, like him, were always up for bucking the system. Dennis became firm friends with John Fashanu and Vinnie Jones, two nutters with reputations as nefarious as his own. The "Crazy Gang" was formed, symbolizing a type of team with a penchant for commando training and a game of astonishing simplicity. Wimbledon soon spread terror across the pitches of the Premier League and won the FA Cup in 1988, beating Liverpool 1–0. "The best moment of my life so far," said Wise.

Always up for a challenge, Wise joined Chelsea in 1990. For eleven seasons, he would apply himself to making the London club one of the most respected and feared of the English elite. His temperament made an impression on everyone, including the Frenchmen Didier Deschamps, Marcel Desailly and Franck Leboeuf, who were, remember, world champions. "Even though he can sometimes be over-committed and his impulsiveness often comes back to bite him, it's Wise that gives the team its tempo," said Deschamps.

Wise became the club's emblem and guiding spirit, and even Ken Bates, Chelsea chairman since 1982, could only congratulate himself on having such a great player. "He's the heartbeat of the club, its driving force. He was here ten years ago, when we were just an average team, only just up from the Second Division. Today, he's still here," he said in 2000.

"When I arrived," Wise observed, "there were so many cliques in the team. The atmosphere wasn't much to speak of and, in terms of diet, preparation and training, anything went. It's the complete opposite now. The club's spirit, resources and ambition are incredible."

Often on the verge of breaking rules on the pitch, Wise clearly broke them when off. In 1995, he was sentenced to three months in prison for beating up and injuring a taxi driver. The sentence was quashed on appeal. "I still had to spend two hours in a cold and dank cell. It was an awful experience that changed my outlook on life like nothing else has," he confirmed. He still continued in the same vein: a one-year driving ban, fines for disciplinary offences and, most memorably, a turbulent and extremely boozy tour of Hong Kong with the England team before Euro 96 – with Paul Gascoigne as ringleader

In August 2002, he was fired by Leicester for "gross misconduct". He was said to have hit his team-mate David Callus in a fight while the team was on tour in Finland in July. It was this inglorious episode that led Wise to join Millwall and its stifling atmosphere. Wise was 35 when he stepped in temporarily as player-manager of the unfashionable club, which had no honours to its name and which had enjoyed just one brief spell in the First Division, from 1988 to 1990.

"When the previous manager was fired, I agreed to take over the team for four matches," he remembered. "Because I won three times, the chairman asked me to stay on permanently." Wise hired Ray Wilkins, whom he knew from his Chelsea days, as his number two, and succeeded in instilling in a fairly ordinary group of players the determination to play and the desire to win. In 2004 Millwall even pulled off an unexpected Cup run, reaching the final against Manchester United. They may not have won the Cup (United won a one-sided match 3–0), but it was still two two fingers up to logic. ∎

Bad boys
Of Football

Patrick Blondeau

Eric Di Meco

Raymond Domenech

Claudio Gentile

Vinnie Jones

Roy Keane

Marco Materazzi

Pedro Monzon

Jose Carlos Mozer

Kevin Muscat

Cyril Rool

Harald Schumacher

Diego Simeone

Patrick Vieira

the real reprobates!!

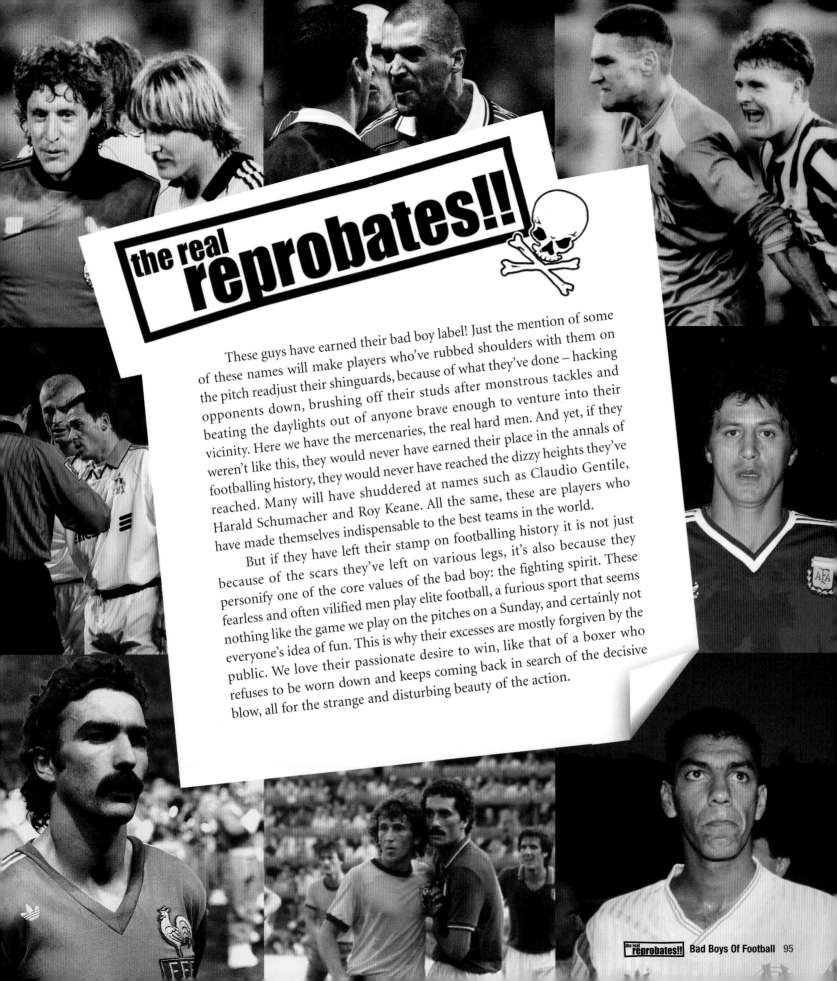

the real reprobates!!

These guys have earned their bad boy label! Just the mention of some of these names will make players who've rubbed shoulders with them on the pitch readjust their shinguards, because of what they've done – hacking opponents down, brushing off their studs after monstrous tackles and beating the daylights out of anyone brave enough to venture into their vicinity. Here we have the mercenaries, the real hard men. And yet, if they weren't like this, they would never have earned their place in the annals of footballing history, they would never have reached the dizzy heights they've reached. Many will have shuddered at names such as Claudio Gentile, Harald Schumacher and Roy Keane. All the same, these are players who have made themselves indispensable to the best teams in the world.

But if they have left their stamp on footballing history it is not just because of the scars they've left on various legs, it's also because they personify one of the core values of the bad boy: the fighting spirit. These fearless and often vilified men play elite football, a furious sport that seems nothing like the game we play on the pitches on a Sunday, and certainly not everyone's idea of fun. This is why their excesses are mostly forgiven by the public. We love their passionate desire to win, like that of a boxer who refuses to be worn down and keeps coming back in search of the decisive blow, all for the strange and disturbing beauty of the action.

Bad boys
Of Football

"I come from Viste, a suburb of Marseille, where you need to know how to defend yourself. That's why I'm hot-headed."

the real reprobates!!

Patrick Blondeau

HIS FISTS DO THE TALKING

the real reprobates!!
Patrick Blondeau

This is the story of a player who built his reputation with his fists. Despite his skill on the ball, Patrick Blondeau is also remembered for notoriously ugly fights. His Mediterranean temperament made the former Monaco and Marseille wing-back hot-headed and fiery – and he doesn't deny it. "It's a question of blood, family … People need to understand where I come from. I come from Viste, a suburb of Marseille, where you have to know how to defend yourself. That's why I'm hot-headed," he said, adding, "When I was young I was an idiot. I only knew force."

During his time at Sheffield Wednesday, Blondeau got involved in several fights with fans. Once, while playing for Olympique Marseille in a UEFA Cup match at Bologna, he head-butted a helmeted Italian policeman, but the player remained as unrepentant as ever. "Everything I do is considered. A fight was breaking out. Peter Luccin was hit from behind and we weren't protected. It was just a case of defending ourselves."

Nor was he averse to the odd "old-school" tackle, one of which, on the Nantes player Yves Deroff, cost Blondeau a one-month suspension and the victim a broken tibia and fibula. At Monaco, he even went for his team-mates. "It was because of stealing," he explained. "Large sums of cash went missing from the dressing-room a number of times during training. After a few months, I worked out who it was. I lost it a bit and I beat up my mates."

But the man from Marseille built his reputation essentially on his intimidation skills. In the tunnel leading from dressing-room to pitch Blondeau was the boss. Opposition players were treated to death-like glares, little shoves with the shoulder and even slaps. Again, Blondeau doesn't mince his words. "There was a famous match against PSG – I didn't lose it – that would have been bad news for Marco Simone – but if there's one thing I can't take it's wind-up merchants, even if they're doing it in Italian. I lived in Monaco and I understand the language pretty well. Idiots and phoney tough-guys need to be sorted out. Not on the pitch, though, in the dressing-room tunnel [laughs]."

In April 2000, during an OM–Monaco match marked by brawls at half-time, the Argentinian Marcelo Gallardo was taken on by the hard wing-back. Half smiling, Blondeau said: "If people get agitated you sometimes have to use intimidation." >

"In Marseille, no one ever comes up to my car shouting 'Bastard!' after a match – no one!"

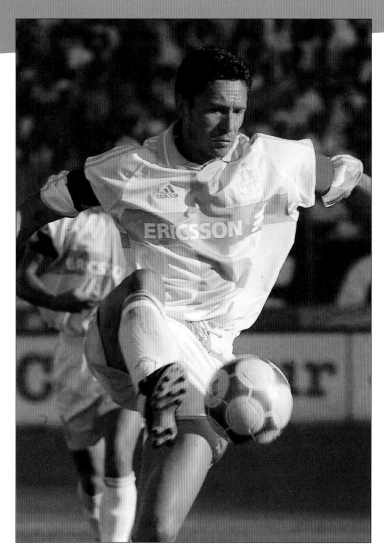

word is his bond!" As long as he felt appreciated by his coach, Blondeau was a priceless asset. He had a unique ability to motivate his team-mates, and would set them straight if he felt they weren't giving enough on a daily basis. "I'm not a bad person but I don't suffer fools. When I think I'm right, I see it through." Beware cheats! "I'm not a big talker, I don't bark orders, I'm more of a protector. I look out for my team-mates." Indeed, Blondeau was always to be found in the front line when temperatures ran high on the pitch. At the same time, despite true commitment to the clubs he played with (Monaco, Bordeaux, Marseille, Creteil), he made the unusual claim of not having much time for other footballers. "You'll never see me hanging out with them for three days in a row. There are a lot of treacherous, self-centred and twisted people in this business."

He admitted to his penchant for nights out in Paris, Monaco and Saint-Tropez. "You'll see me in a club three days before a match. I like nice cars too. I've never hidden any of this. There are no limits for me, I love life too much," he said, adding, "I'm not an example. I don't sleep much; I don't have an athlete's diet. They say you need a certain lifestyle to stay fit through the season, but I don't see it that way. In my defence, I don't drink, I don't smoke cigarettes and I've never smoked weed."

We are left with a contradictory image. On the one hand a defender who, without necessarily being gifted from the outset, has achieved a respectable haul of trophies (French champion in 1997, UEFA Cup finalist in 1999, part of the national team twice). On the other hand, a "big-shot" who might well have gone off the rails if it hadn't been for football. Let's not forget, either, the Blondeau who sometimes loses control on the pitch, who upholds his "reputation" through sometimes astonishing declarations.

"I'm quite an odd bloke, unmanageable," he says in an amusing self-portrait. "I hardly ever get letters from chicks saying 'You're so good-looking', it's more like 'You're a poet, a weirdo…'" Then, as if aware that he is wandering from the point and anxious not to reveal too much, he returns to his favourite subject, his supposed machismo. "Some people think I'm a cold person. Give me that any day rather than people patting my head or ruffling my hair all the time when I'm out. I want permanent respect." Or: "In Marseille, no one ever comes up to my car shouting 'Bastard!' after a match – no one!"

Straight-talking, charming, irritating, anti-authority, irritated by injustice, Blondeau sums himself up as follows: "I'm strong-minded but I don't get nasty." It's good to have that clarified. ∎

Blondeau also used intimidation on reporters if he wasn't happy about an article. To get a better understanding of his strong-arm tactics, you need to look to those around him. His spiritual fathers were, in fact, Rolland Courbis and Francis "the Belgian", a Marseille mafia boss and the victim of a revenge killing in 2000. Blondeau was one of the coffin bearers at his funeral. We also see in Blondeau some of the "values" so typical of this background: honour, friendship and, above all, a merciless attitude towards the enemy.

This loyalty sometimes got him involved in senseless fights, but it was also his strength. "I'm straight, I don't sidestep the issue. Anyone will tell you, I'm totally loyal and extremely generous. For me, a man's

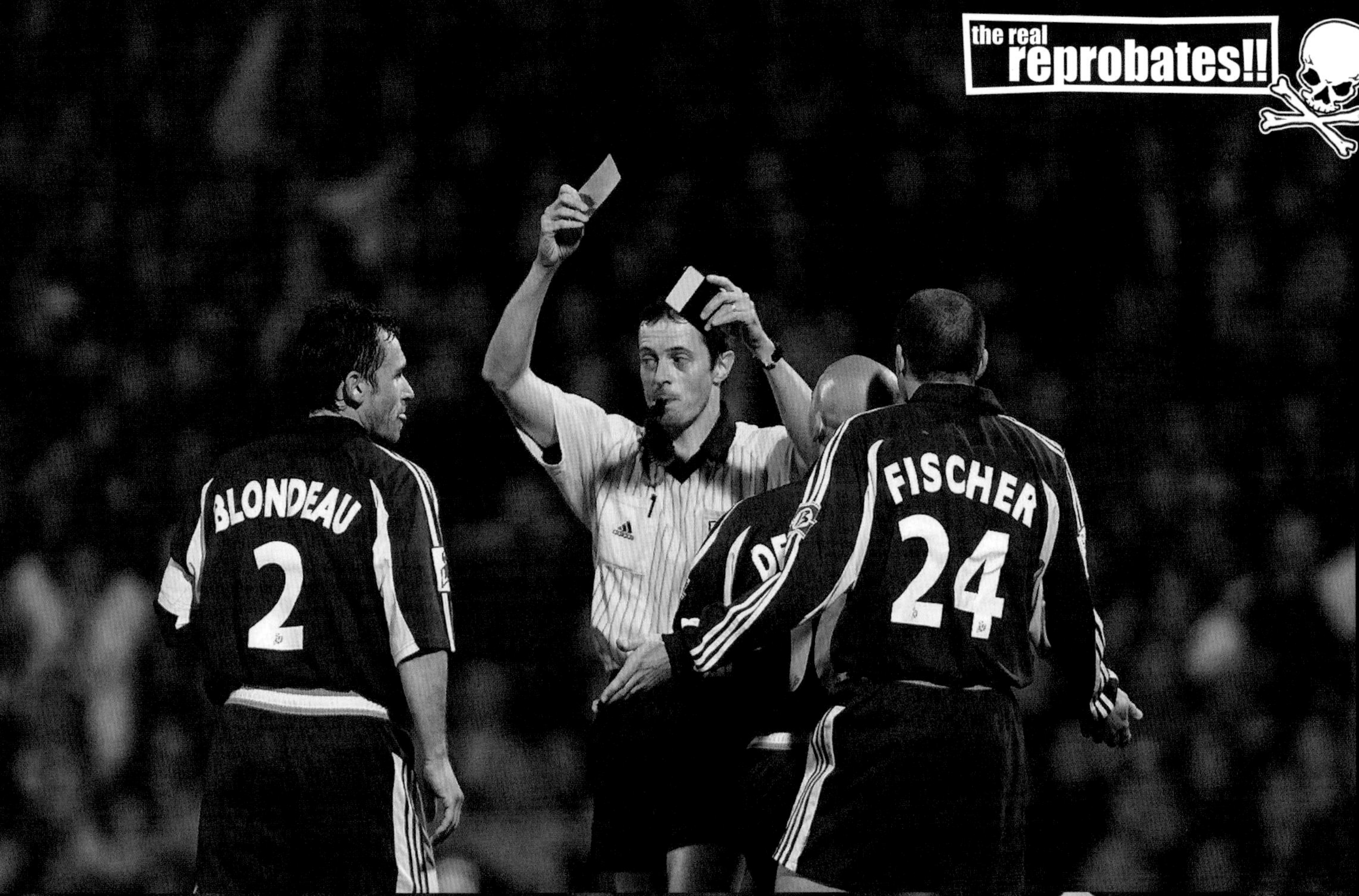
BLONDEAU
2
FISCHER
24

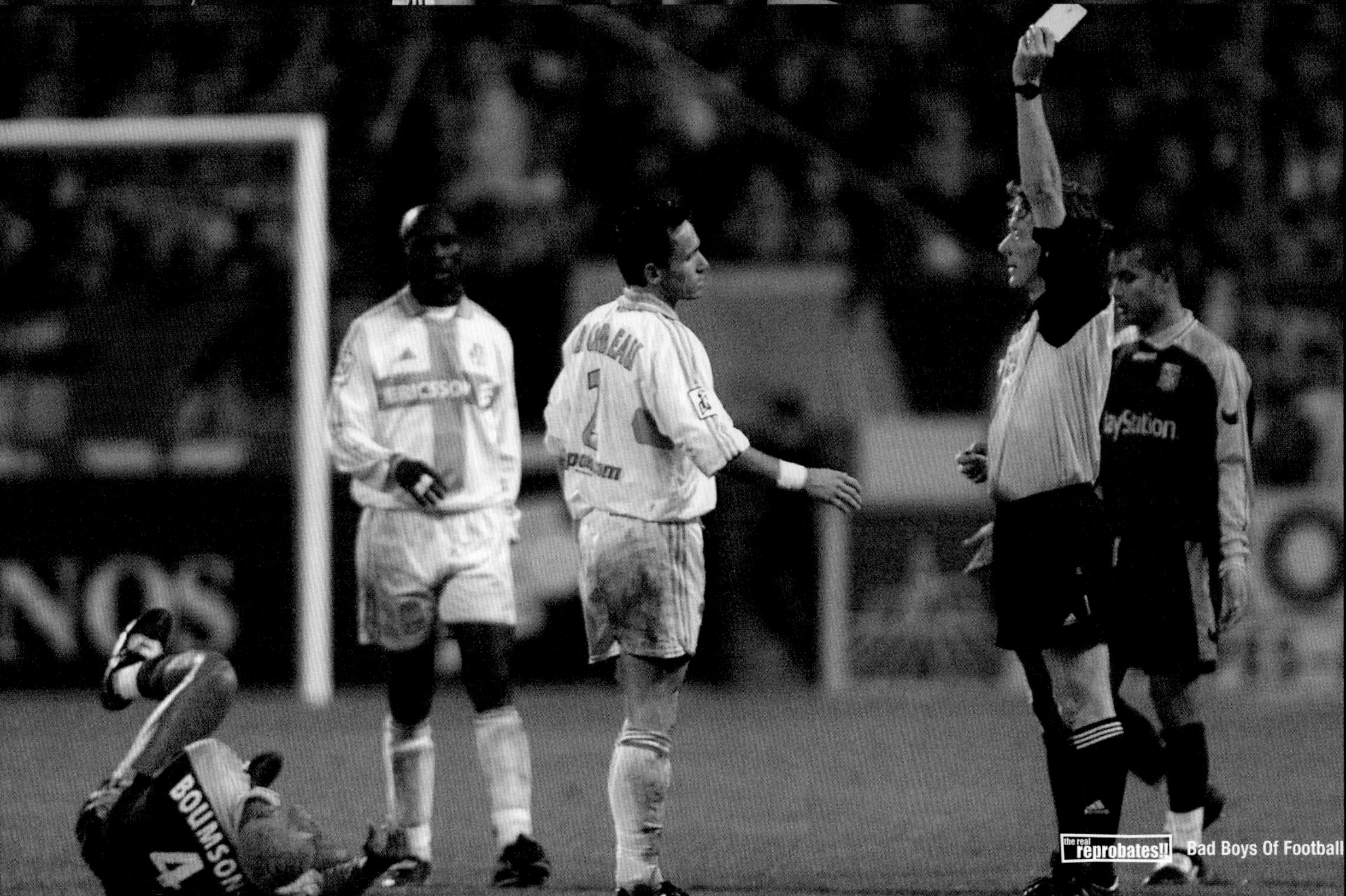
BOUMSON

Eric Di Meco

THE BIG-HEARTED TACKLER

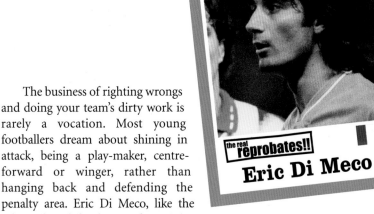

the real
reprobates!!
Eric Di Meco

"**Image problem? I've got a big one. It's like wrestling, there are good guys and bad guys. I'm one of the bad guys.**"

The business of righting wrongs and doing your team's dirty work is rarely a vocation. Most young footballers dream about shining in attack, being a play-maker, centre-forward or winger, rather than hanging back and defending the penalty area. Eric Di Meco, like the others, shared the dream. The training centre of his all-time favourite club, Olympic Marseille, had plans for the Avignon boy as a future left-winger. But if he'd stayed in this position, he would certainly have been confined to a modest career in the second division, along with most of the other "Minots" – the generation of young players who trained at the club, some of whom took Marseille to the top flight in 1984.

It was Arsene Wenger who started the transformation. He trialled Di Meco as a wing-back during his time at Nancy over the 1986–87 season. But it was Gerard Banide who completed it when Eric returned to the Marseille fold after a disappointing loan spell at Martigues. Bordering on depressed, on the verge of quitting football, the former winger had no choice. He accepted the unfamiliar role, little suspecting that this would make him one of the most successful players in French football, with five French League titles (or six if you include the title that Marseille was stripped of in 1993 for corruption), one European Cup (1993, following a final appearance in 1991) and one French Cup.

No more supporting roles for this hot-headed footballer with the long mane of black hair. Banide's strategy transformed an unproductive winger into a respected international and a terror in the domestic game, one of the bad boys featured on TV trailers for the French league championship in the 1990s. In no time at all, his spectacular long-range tackles and his extraordinary commitment became both indispensable and a liability. Michel Platini, who took over the reins of the French squad in 1988 from Henri Michel in order to prepare for Euro 92, and who didn't miss a trick, entrusted him with the role on the left of the team's defence. Di Meco wore the French shirt on 23 occasions and never lost a match, notching up 18 victories and five draws.

Despite his trophies, the player remained, or so thought the fans at the time, a rough, even violent defender, although he had never inflicted a single serious injury. This can be explained by the fact that the emergence of the former Marseille "Minot" coincided with the Tapie era and the start of the over-the-top hostility between OM and Paris St Germain. During this period of rivalry, which was skilfully perpetuated by the media around their clashes in the League, Di Meco was one of the key players. In December 1992, in a match won by Marseille at Parc des Princes (1–0), a particularly forceful tackle on Laurent Fournier (who had "started it", according to his opponent), provided ammunition that rival fans would go on using for years. The power of image … Di Meco was never under any illusions. "Image problem? I've got a big one. It's like wrestling, there are good guys and bad guys. I'm one of the bad guys. It's true I never do anything by halves, but it's always with the intention of winning the ball. For me, it's never been a question of wrong intent and I've never hurt anyone. In the end I accepted my reputation and made the most of it," he said on his retirement in 1998.

Across the pitches in France, and despite his faultless performances in the national squad, Di Meco was booed by rival fans. His reputation, now firmly established, had a dual effect. On the one hand, he admits, as time went on attacking players tended increasingly to steer clear of his famous sliding tackles. On the other, he believes that his bad guy image may have damaged his international career. Here too, his reputation was indelibly tarnished by a sending-off during his third international match against Scotland (a 3–0 win for France in October 1989) after a brutal charge on Mo Johnston. After Platini, Aime Jacquet kept confidence in him, and even gave him the captain's armband. Throughout the Gerard Houllier era, however, he was to be left in the international wilderness.

For the "Minot" who'd come of age, the epilogue doesn't match up to the giddy Marseille years. He was transferred to Monaco in 1994, and although he was a League title winner again with the Principality club in 1997, his decline had already begun. In 1996 he began to be supplanted in the French team by the young Bixente Lizarazu, and then came a serious knee injury. The ponytail that became his trademark towards the end of his career is fondly remembered by all OM fans, in whose eyes the former defender had become one of Marseille's national treasures. The largest Marseille fan group, the Winners, officially changed its name to "the Friends of Di Meco" …

Always a devoted and loyal player, Di Meco remained passionately attached to the club and the city, and is an example of one who has had a successful life after football. Following his retirement, Di Meco joined the municipal team of the mayor of Marseille, Jean-Claude Gaudin, leading projects for kids from disadvantaged areas, and showing the same authority and selflessness that drove him as a player. ■

"I was making my debut and thought it was important to get people talking about me, positively or negatively. It was a sort of bravado. I went into character."

the real reprobates!!

Raymond Domenech

the real reprobates!!

THE BORN ACTOR

Raymond Domenech

Could it be that the hard man defender and the confrontational coach both came about in the same way, through a misunderstanding? It was only because of an incident on the pitch for which Raymond Domenech was unfairly blamed that his reputation as a hard man was born. And, paradoxically, it was because he was more affable and more cooperative with the press than his predecessors that Domenech and the media gradually grew further and further apart.

On August 12, 1970, the first day of the season, Olympic Lyon went to Nice and lost 2–0. When the Austrian player Helmut Metzler burst through for Nice, he took the ball past a young defender, Raymond Domenech (who was 18 but looked five years older), and was then smashed into by the last Lyon defender, Jean Baeza. The Nice forward collapsed to the ground, his tibia and fibula fractured. His career was over. Although he had nothing to do with it, Domenech was identified as the guilty party, and was immediately labelled an assassin. This is where his personality becomes more complex. He didn't really attempt to refute the claim. "Baeza and I had the same haircut. The reporters got us confused and blamed me for the tackle. I did nothing to put them straight. I was making my debut and thought it was important to get people talking about me, positively or negatively. It was a sort of bravado. I went into character."

Although wrongly accused, he then did everything possible to ensure that his appearance and his behaviour matched his reputation. To accompany his famous moustache, he grew a black beard, obscuring his face and making his intelligent expression stand out. (He would shave this moustache off the day he stopped playing.) The following season, again at Nice, he tackled Charly Loubet from behind and picked up a deserved red card at the beginning of the second half. Because the match was televised, the myth took hold. In 1973, at home against Marseille in the quarter-finals of the French Cup, he copped a punch from Skoblar (he still has the scar!), but it was Domenech that the Marseille fans booed because he'd previously trampled on the Marseille striker. On another occasion, he brought down Christian Sarramagna, who was carried off, his ankle sprained in two places. The St Etienne player himself believed it was an accident. "Raymond made his presence felt, but didn't do anything wrong because he was always well positioned." Domenech, on the other hand, didn't mind offering a bit of verbal provocation, more often than not to the crowd, especially the St Etienne fans. The result was predictable. "I was watched closely by the referees, I was a marked man, so when I tackled, even when it was by the book, I was whistled at by the fans and by the referee. When tempers run a bit high, it's Domenech who gets the yellow card, just to restore calm. I'm not a saint, but I'm no harder than the others." >

"When I was a player, if we'd been 3–0 down with two minutes left, and someone needed to be chopped in half, I would have done it."

Maybe so, but he's far more cunning and inflammatory than that. There's nothing discreet about Domenech, who is about as direct as a punch in the face. "If you make football your career, you have to quickly learn how to be a mercenary and change your 18-year-old mentality so you don't end up out on the streets, because you only have ten years or so in which to provide for your future." At Strasburg, where he spent four seasons between 1977 and 1981 and won the League championship in 1979, he said straight off: "I don't feel like an Alsatian, I have very little contact with Alsatian people."

At the age of 28, he got his coaching badges, coming through top of his class. He said then that he was sure he would want to coach one day, "but not in an amateur or even a Second Division club". After winning the French Cup with Bordeaux in 1984, he resigned himself to the fact that he was increasingly prone to injury and decided to take the plunge. He became player/coach of Mulhouse, in Division Two, and then, following more injuries, just the coach. He explained his methodology: "I'll listen to everyone but I'll only take notice of opinions I consider worth hearing." He did what he said and didn't mind offending people. Twenty years later, as the national team coach, he would say virtually the same thing. In response to those who questioned his decisions before the 2006 World Cup, he arranged a meeting for July 9, the day of the final. And he was there – for his biggest disappointment, when they drew 1–1 with Italy and lost 5–3 on penalties. "It's still a failure for me. I've never been able to accept defeat. When I was a player, if we'd been 3–0 down with two minutes left, and someone needed to be chopped in half, I would have done it."

After Mulhouse, he managed Lyon between 1988 and 1993 and then joined the French technical team, where he took charge of the French youth team. Ever the amateur comedian, he used tricks of the theatre trade to encourage his players to express themselves, drawing on surprise, charm and disruption. He didn't attempt to hide his interest in astrology, scorning those who mocked him for it and even fuelling the derision. At the start of his managerial career he insisted that he would never be influenced by the star signs of his players when it came to team selection. On becoming the national coach, however, he actually said about Pires and Pedretti: "Scorpions always end up killing each other." Manna from heaven for his critics.

In 2002, he was approached about succeeding Roger Lemerre as manager of the French national team, but it was Santini who got the job. Two years later, Aime Jacquet appointed Domenech. Although he was received positively by the media at first, it wasn't long before he drove them mad. He would answer questions with questions, give monosyllabic replies, even reprimand his questioners, revelling in the exasperation he caused. He was convinced that there was no point in explaining himself, that however much he talked he'd only be misunderstood, so he ended up not even trying, or even – the ultimate paradox – asking them to be more critical. And letting the results speak for themselves. ■

Claudio Gentile

THE DEVIL WHO DEVOURED MARADONA

"We aren't at dance school, we play football!"

What would God be without the Devil? Not much. It's through the effect of contrast that the "reprobates" of football have built their bad reputation. All of them, on their day, have stifled one of the great world players, annihilated talent, even genius. Diego Maradona's dark shadow, anti-genius or *bête noire* was, without doubt, Claudio Gentile. When Argentina and Italy met in the second group phase of the 1982 World Cup in Spain, "El Pibe de Oro" was hunted so persistently by Gentile that he stood out only by his almost total absence in a match won 2–1 by Italy.

No "Hand of God" this time for Diego, unlike the one in 1986 that would see his team knock England out before going on to win the supreme title (see page 37). On this occasion it was the feet of the Devil and a walk in the wilderness for the Argentine genius, orchestrated by "Gaddafi", the nickname given to Gentile, the guy from Tripoli, Libya, whose name is close to "gentle" but whose play is far from it.

In the same finals competition, Gentile nullified Zico of Brazil (who were beaten 3–2) and later Karl-Heinz Rummenigge of Germany (beaten in the final, 3–1). Although we're more likely to remember Paolo Rossi or Marco Tardelli, the Azurri owe their third World Cup to a large extent to their resilient defender, a living symbol of the Italian *catenaccio* tactical system – taken, in his case, to the point of caricature.

In every match, his direct adversary was subjected to a nightmare, in an era when forwards were far less protected than they are today. Kicks to ankles and calves, incessant shirt-pulling, shoulder barging, rough tackles – he had the whole repertoire and used it.

As a result, we often forget that Gentile was also a lively and sharp counter-attacker, always ready to retrieve the ball from deep in his area and tease his opponents before delivering an accurate cross. For this devilish player, the road to hell was paved with good intentions. One of his retorts has gone down in history. "We aren't at dance school, we play football!" was his defence of his ruthless job on Maradona, during which all he picked up was a yellow card, ruling him out of the semi-final against Poland (which Italy won 2–0).

Claudio Gentile

Like most industrious and opinionated defenders, Gentile was far from being an artist, and made up for his lack of individual talent with hard work (he watched tapes of Maradona for several days in order to pinpoint his weaknesses), an intense drive to do well, an all-or-nothing attitude and an incredible dogged determination. This unshakeable desire to win undoubtedly stems from his childhood spent playing with other sons of Italian migrants and the young Libyan boys on the dusty streets of his native Tripoli.

When his family were forced out by the Libyan authorities and moved back to Italy, young Claudio was still only eight but had already been bitten by the football bug.

After training at Arona and then at Varese, the young guy from Libya with the curly black hair went on to become a linchpin of the Juventus side, wearing the black-and-white shirt of "the Old Lady" on 414 occasions and winning six League titles, a UEFA Cup and a European Cup Winners Cup.

And, underlining the fact that the bad boys are often essentially men of conscience who are forced to do their team's dirty work, a few years after his retirement as a player Gentile committed himself wholeheartedly to training and coaching, just like Raymond Domenech. From 2000 to 2002, he was the right-hand man of his former Juve boss Giovanni Trapattoni, who was at the helm of the Italian team. He then coached the Italian youth team, a team that won bronze in the 2004 Athens Olympics (the first Italian Olympic medal for football for 68 years), won five out of seven European Under-21 Championships between 1992 and 2004, and made the final stages of the 2006 and 2007 Championships in Portugal and Holland. "Having a strong image as a player and authority makes it easier to pass on the message to young players," he explained.

There was also a price to pay for his selfless devotion to no-nonsense football. In 1990, at the end of his career as a player, he quit the world of football completely to "dry out" in a textiles company for four years. Only then did the Devil return to try his luck … ∎

"I'm Vinnie Jones, I'm a gipsy, I make a packet. I'll tear your ear off with my teeth then spit it out on the grass."

Vinnie Jones

THE BUSINESSMAN GLADIATOR

"They're gonna put me in the movies, they're gonna make a big star out of me. We'll make a film about a man that's sad and lonely, and all I gotta do is act naturally!"

Vinnie Jones loves to quote "Act Naturally" (one of Ringo Starr's rare moments of glory as a singer), recorded by the Beatles in 1965, as the song that best sums up his life. The imposing Welshman certainly didn't have to undergo any transformation to become what he is today: the very embodiment of the bad boy, and the one who gets the most media coverage in the UK and the whole planet of football. With a real gift for business, an exceptional talent for publicity stunts and lucrative partnerships, Vinnie Jones has turned his bad reputation into a going concern.

Many people have made the leap between sport and showbiz, from Rod Stewart (former apprentice footballer) to Yannick Noah and of course Eric Cantona. The former Wimbledon midfielder, however, opted for a more traditional approach, starting out by playing musclemen of few words, a little like the French stars Lino Ventura,

Vinnie Jones

formerly a wrestler, or Michel Constantin, former volleyball international. Then, little by little, he extended his range, and the bad boy became a full-time actor. Soon he was getting lead roles, as in *Mean Machine*, in which he plays footballer Johnny Was, as well as supporting roles in major productions such as *X-Men 3*.

The truth is there's nothing that complex about Vinnie, this kid from Watford who, at the age of 16, left his broken home to go and live his life. He tended and polished his bad boy image, even calling his autobiography, published in 1998, *Confessions of a Bad Boy*. Scandal and a bit of luck did the rest ...

Jones's explosion on to the front pages of the tabloid press was, in fact, largely brought about by the Football Association. By punishing him for producing his video compilation *Soccer's Hard Men* (released in 1992), it gave the number-one advocate of rough football an unintentional helping hand. A record fine of £20,000 was completely derisory compared with the money he made from the video. >

"At one point, he spat in my face and said: 'I'm just going to take the corner, but don't worry, fat boy, I'll be back!'"

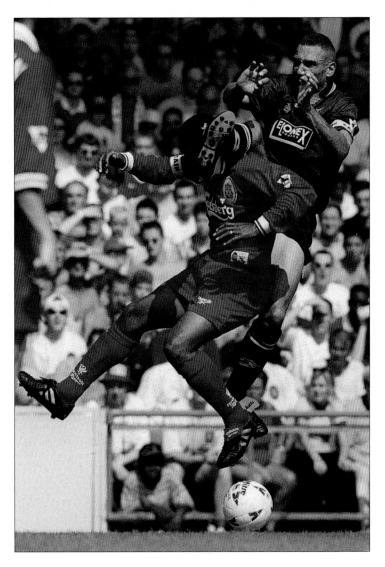

It was a stroke of luck for Jones that English cinema was seeing a new craze for thug and gangster films at the time. Film-makers were therefore on the lookout for proper hard men, and Vinnie Jones stood out. He made his debut with the role of Big Chris in *Lock, Stock and Two Smoking Barrels*, the first film by Madonna's husband Guy Ritchie, and went on to play another 15 or so characters in films in which he paraded his no-nonsense bulk and heeded Ringo Starr's advice to "act naturally".

His personality, however, caused him problems in real life and his temper got him into trouble with the law on two occasions. In 1998, right in the middle of filming with Guy Ritchie, he was sentenced to one hundred hours of community service after being found guilty of violently assaulting a neighbour. The court ordered him to assist the elderly, an experience, he said, that opened his eyes to their plight. Five years later, he was convicted for a violent air rage offence, a misdemeanour that led one of his sponsors, a brand of rum, to break their advertising contract.

Jones has made such progress in his acting career that you almost forget that this improbable international, who even captained the Welsh team (he had a grandfather from Wales), played 486 League matches and won the Cup in 1998 with Wimbledon, beating Liverpool 1–0 in one of the great Cup final upsets of recent years. Wimbledon was and always would be the club of Vincent Peter Jones, but he also played at Leeds, Sheffield United and Chelsea before ending his career as player-manager at Queen's Park Rangers. Legend has it that at Wimbledon he thought nothing of pinning up against the wall any team-mate who didn't show enough devotion to the shirt.

Despite being called up nine times for Wales and his Cup victory, his most famous footballing moment remains his *very* tight marking of Paul Gascoigne, another bad boy in the making (see page 30), during a match against Newcastle in 1988. The photo (see opposite) of this dubious passage of play spread across the world. The foundations of Vinnie Jones's bad reputation had been laid … Gazza commented after the match: "He came up to me and said: 'I'm Vinnie Jones, I'm a gipsy, I make a packet. I'll tear your ear off with my teeth then spit it out on the grass. It's just you and me today, fat boy!' I constantly felt his breath behind me, like a dragon. I was never scared about being tackled, but with this guy, it was just one assault after another! At one point, he spat in my face and said: 'I'm just going to take the corner, but don't worry, fat boy, I'll be back!'"

His friends, however, like to talk about the unpublicized side of Vinnie, about the man who's actively involved in children's charities and who donated most of his fee for *Lock, Stock and Two Smoking Barrels* to the hospital that carried out a successful heart transplant on his wife Tanya. Guy Ritchie once said of Jones: "If there were an apocalypse, a number of things would survive … Vinnie Jones would be one of them!" ∎

Vinnie Jones

"I've tangled with so many people that before a match, I don't know who I should be shaking hands with any more."

Roy Keane

Roy Keane

THE WAR MONGER

In the category of outright villains, terrifying bad boys, fearless hard men, Roy Keane stands alone. He had had a tough childhood and he was not going to let anyone grab his place, or the ball, on a football pitch …

From Mayfield, a working-class area of Cork, Roy was the son of a worker who, like so many in Ireland, worked on and off at Guinness. Roy soon discovered that he was not much interested in school work, and that for him the key to success lay in sport. He tried several, including boxing, which he was involved in from the age of 12. He even took part in four fights in the Novice League, but finally opted for football. "I immediately felt comfortable. Boxing gave me a lot of confidence in the face of physical aggression," he once said. From then on he did everything he could to get noticed, using any means, not least his drive and phenomenal lung capacity. He played at local club Rockmount AFC, and hoped to turn professional, but his dreams were shattered when, at the age of 15, he was overlooked for the national youth team. It was all the more disappointing because four of his team-mates were picked.

He was not one to give up, however. Certain that, for him, it was football or nothing, he offered his services to the clubs in the north of England, only to be disappointed again. He was not technical enough, they said … He then signed for a semi-professional Irish team, Cobh Ramblers. He may have been prepared to go abroad to make a living, but Keane was still an Irishman through and through, and a proud one too, with a tattoo of the Celtic cross on his left bicep, and names of his five children on the right.

In 1990, at the age of 19, he spotted in a Cup match by Nottingham Forest. The day after his first match at Forest, Brian Clough, the manager, made him polish his shoes. Humbly, Keane did as he was told … The following away match was at Liverpool, and the youngster thought he was only there to carry the gear, but, one hour

before kick-off, Clough handed him a shirt. He would be a Forest regular for three years. When he transferred to Manchester United in 1993, the transfer deal was impressive for a defensive player (in the region of £4,000,000). He figured in Alex Ferguson's plans to conquer the world – and Keane would make it happen. In a team containing Cantona, Giggs, Gary Neville, Schmeichel, Stam and Beckham, he established himself as the skipper. It was Keane who set the tone of the matches. It was often Keane who committed the first foul. "I have to show the opponent, right from the start, that if he wants a physical fight, I'll be ready. Throwing in the first tackle is the best way of getting the message across."

He picked up his first red card in 1995, during a Cup semi-final against Crystal Palace, after failing to keep his temper in check with Gareth Southgate, a name synonymous with fair play. From then, the bad boy label stuck, and he'd work hard to justify it. In 1997, drunk in a hotel at 4.30 a.m., two days before a match at Leeds, he started a pitched battle. He had a bad game at Elland Road and, five minutes before the end of normal time, tore the cruciate ligament in his knee when attempting to tackle the Leeds player, Alf Inge Haaland. "Get up, cheat, stop taking the piss!" said the Norwegian scathingly. Keane wouldn't forget. Bryan Robson, the emblematic ex-Manchester United player, someone who knew all about killer tackles and score settling, advised him that revenge was a dish best served cold. "Wait and see, one day you'll catch up with him. Be patient …" It was around this time that Keane began abusing the Guinness. "I drank much too much," he admitted, and he smashed up too many pubs. Each time Ferguson covered for him. "I owe everything to Sir Alex. He knew how to divert the fakers and bullshitters. He's always been there for me, especially when my life was upside down. He didn't want a boy scout. He accepts me as I am, good, bad or nasty." >

"When I'm on holiday, it's the monster people see in me … They probably think that Roy Keane must dish out as much punishment to his kids …"

Thanks to Roy Keane, Manchester United would pull off a magnificent treble in 1999 – the Cup, the League title and the Champions League. Keane, however, only played twelve minutes in the 2–0 FA Cup final victory against Newcastle, after receiving an ankle injury from Gary Speed. He promised he'd come and find him, but it turned out that it would be the tabloid press that found Keane, at the heart of a new scandal. Having rubbed two women up the wrong way – they complained that he had refused to buy them a drink – he got into yet another fight in a Manchester pub. He was glassed in the eye and ended up in custody, news that did not escape the *Sun*.

In the cell, Keane sobered up and slept off his shame. "I thought about my wife and children. Then I thought about the club and the upcoming matches, the most important in United's history, while its captain's making himself ill through drink. Getting myself caught up in this business of birds, drink and fights before a Champions League final, even if I was suspended [due to a stupid tackle on Zidane in the semi-final against Juventus], proves that I'm just a dickhead. Keane the savage, no excuse!"

From then on, he kept his nose clean – off the pitch. Charming when he hadn't been drinking, he seemed surprised that his deadly reputation preceded him. "When I'm on holiday, it's the monster people see in me. They stare at me by the pool eating ice creams and having fun with my kids and they seem amazed. They probably think that Roy Keane must dish out as much punishment to his kids …"

Tony Cascarino, another Irish (but British-born) footballer of international repute, believed that Keane was someone to be careful with. "Roy Keane scares everyone. Even Alex Ferguson's scared of him!" But it was with Ferguson that Keane experienced his finest years. English League champion seven times, he also won the Cup four times and was voted 2000 Player of the Year by his peers. He clocked up an average of twelve yellow and two red cards a year.

Then came April 21, 2001, and the Manchester derby. Finally Keane did indeed catch up with Haaland, who had now moved to Manchester City. At the first opportunity, he hurled himself at the player and shattered his leg … It was clearly a pre-meditated tackle and an attempt to injure. Keane didn't even wait for the red card to be shown. He turned his back and returned to the dressing-room, but not before spitting venomously in Haaland's face, whose career was also now shattered. Remorse? Not likely! "I'd waited long enough. I fucking hit him hard. Take that you ****! And don't ever stand over me again sneering about fake injuries!" This account would be sanitized in his book, *The Autobiography*, which was published in 2002 and sold 400,000 copies.

Keane was fined £150,000 and was suspended for five matches, although he didn't understand what all the fuss was about. "Late tackles are part and parcel of football." The Irishman, on the other hand, couldn't stand players who pulled shirts or lashed out behind the referee's back, and most of all he hated diving. >

"With me, it's all attitude."

When Thierry Henry took a stand against racism in January 2005 and, together with his sponsor, launched a black-and-white "Stand up, speak up" bracelet, Keane replied by proposing a "No diving" bracelet, pouring scorn on the Premier League divers. Keane had little time for the aesthetes of football, team-mates or not, and once described Beckham as just "a work colleague".

"I'm a player with limited qualities, but at least I know that. I would never try and dribble the ball past two or three players to score. I don't know how to do it. I win the ball and pass it to people who know how to play. I've done that my whole career. My attitude is my strength. With me, it's all attitude." He demonstrated this on February 1, 2005, at Highbury, in a classic League game between Arsenal and Manchester United. Things were getting heated between Patrick Vieira and Gary Neville in the corridor. A furious Roy Keane pushed forward and said: "If you want to fight, don't pick on the small ones. Come and have a go at me!" Vieira remembered the incident: "Keane behaved in exactly the same way I would have done if he'd just spoken to an Arsenal player. When I started out in the English league, Keane was the player I wanted to measure myself against, because he was the best in his position. I've the greatest respect for him."

Winner of this duel (United won 4–2), Keane also won himself a fan. In the main, however, he caused trouble but didn't let it trouble him. "I've tangled with so many people that before a match, I don't know who I should be shaking hands with any more." In the meantime, Roy Keane had become a phenomenon in Ireland. Morrissey, former lead singer with the Smiths, dedicated a play and its title to the footballer. Called *I, Keano*, it was staged in Dublin and also played at Cork, where he was born. It recounted, in detail, how Keane was booted out of the Irish squad before the 2002 World Cup. On centre stage in Japan, Keane had abandoned his team-mates and hurled insults at the then manager Mick McCarthy, notably calling him an "English ****". It took an Irishman, Brian Kerr, to convince him to change his mind in May 2004 and take part in the qualifying rounds of the 2006 World Cup. Keane would be called up to the national team a total of 66 times and score nine goals for Ireland.

Rather than finish on a bad note, Keane precipitated the end of his career at United. In 2005, he gave an explosive interview to Manchester United TV, in which he blasted a number of team-mates; he even turned on Alex Ferguson. The time had come for him to leave the club at which he'd spent 12 years, and in December 2005 he joined Celtic. After an injury-plagued six months in Glasgow he retired in June 2006. Alex Ferguson bore no grudge and paid his own tribute: "Roy was obsessed with winning and that made him a great captain." Keane shed a tear or two at his testimonial, during which he was applauded by the 69,000-strong Old Trafford crowd who had come to salute their bad-boy hero, and living legend. But Keane was back in football quickly, as manager of Sunderland, working for former Republic of Ireland team-mate Niall Quinn. He took over in September 2007 and won the championship in his first season. ∎

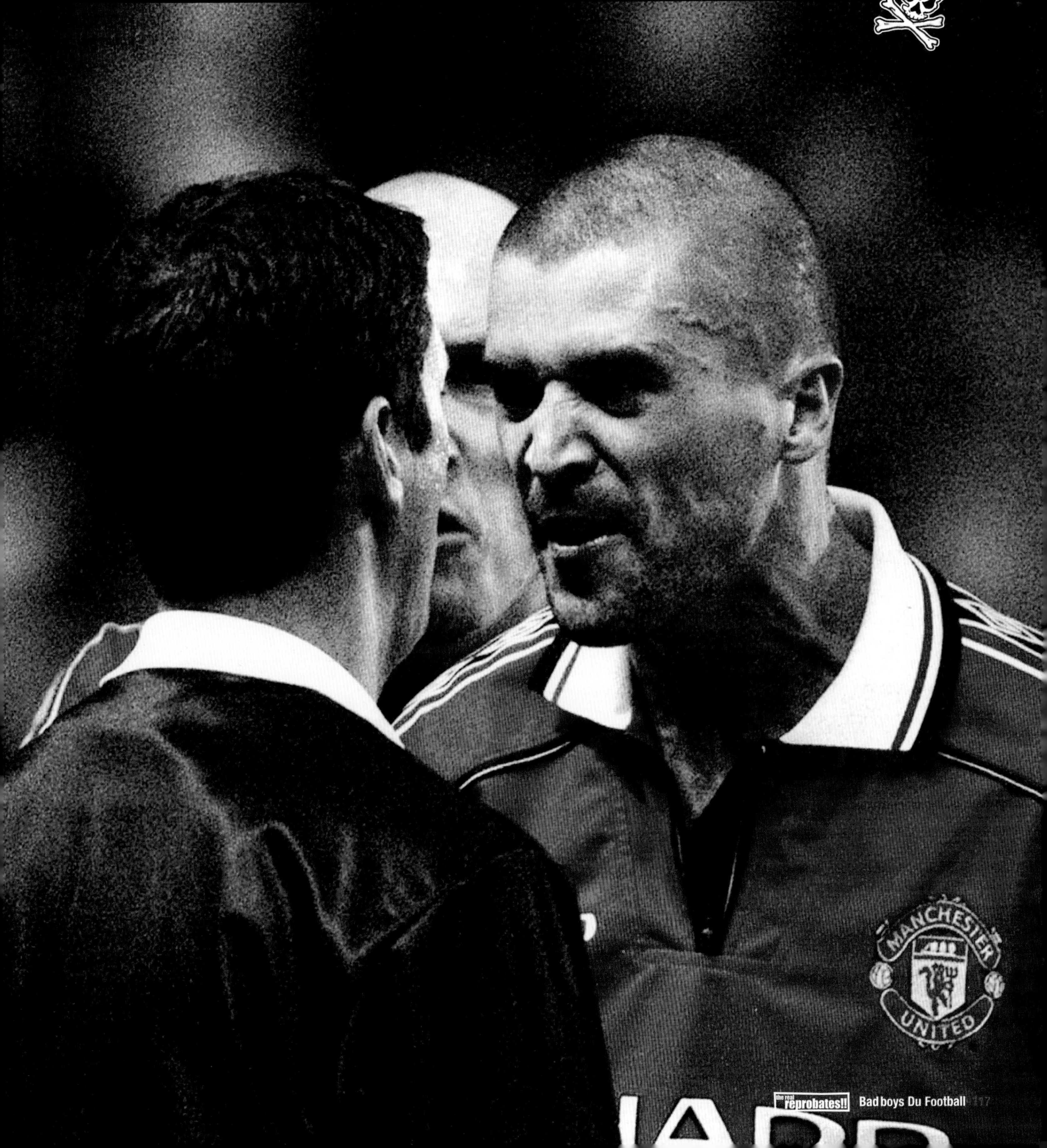
MANCHESTER
UNITED

"In football, there have always been some things that are settled on the pitch."

Marco Materazzi

THE PLAYER WITH *THAT* CHEST

the real reprobates!!

Marco Materazzi

In a split second, Marco Materazzi's destiny changed. Thanks to the most famous head-butt in the history of football, the player who might never have been anything more than just another industrious player of the Calcio, the latest in a long line of rugged Italian defenders, became an international superstar, an advertising tool advertisers fell over themselves to bid for. It would, however, be unfair to judge Marco Materazzi solely on the 2006 World Cup final, and to see him just as a rough and ready wind-up merchant whose only claim to fame is that he succeeded, as many had before him, in making Zinedine Zidane lose the plot. No, the Inter Milan defender has proved far more than that.

His own World Cup performance is worth a little look. He was first of all presented with a gem of a red card in Italy's 1–0 victory over Australia in the second round of the knockout stage, following a characteristic late tackle on Bresciano. Then, in the seventh minute of the final, one of his fouls on Florent Malouda caused the Squadra to concede a penalty and allowed Zinedine Zidane to open the scoring.

"Matrix", as he is pejoratively known by fans of Inter's rivals, is also good with his head. He'd already scored a headed goal in the 26th minute of Italy's first-round game against the Czech Republic, which they won 2–0, only nine minutes after coming on as substitute for injured Nesta. And in the final against France it was Matarazzi who equalized, again with his head, in the 19th minute. That's the kind of player Marco is. As he says himself, "I'm not technically gifted like some of the great Italian defenders, but I give everything on the pitch." >

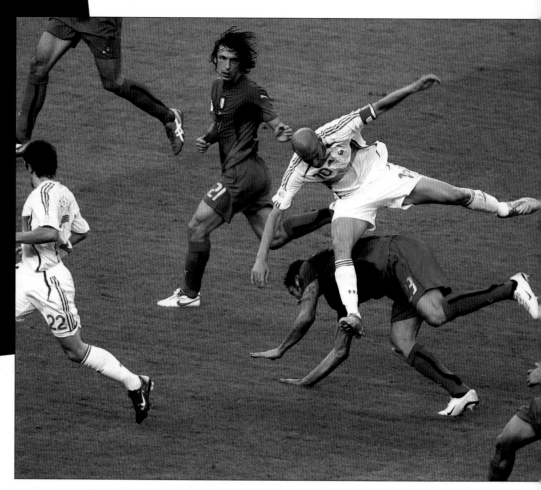

> The two-match suspension he picked up for verbally provoking the French captain was, in his view, "an affront, not only to me, but to the world of football."

His character was forged in six years of sparring in Italy's second, third and fourth divisions between 1990 and 1996. In his early days in Serie A, at Perugia, he was memorably teamed with Gennaro Gattuso (see page 66). For a while the two terrors even shared a flat. A useful opportunity to exchange some technical thoughts on the use of elbows, sliding tackles, thumps in the back, tackles from behind ... To fine-tune his mental strength, Materazzi spent the 1998–99 season in exile in England, at Everton, without great success. On his return to Perugia, however, he set about scoring goals (his tally of 12 in 2000–01 was an Italian record for a central defender), earning himself a lucrative transfer to Inter.

It was at Milan that he showed everyone what he was capable of. His trophy list includes: Zlatan Ibrahimovic's right ankle (October 2005) during a Serie A match between Inter and Juve; Fabio Cannavaro's head during an Azzurri training session (October 2006) and Christian Vieri's thigh during another national squad training session (February 2006); he also smashed the face of Pablo Sorin in the Champions League quarter-final second leg against Villareal in April 2006 ... To this we can add Andrei Chevtchenko's cartilage, Filippo Inzaghi's ankle, Vieri's knee and Bruno Cirillo's lower lip, the Siena player having received a clout in the tunnel on the way to the pitch. In 2002 he came to blows with Alessandro Nesta before a match at Rome, the same Nesta that he would substitute in the 2006 World Cup match against the Czech Republic.

Although he accepted his punishment each time and claimed to have calmed down, Marco was secretly quite proud of himself. After Zidane's head-butt to his chest, he played the victim, claiming that he expected an apology from the Frenchman. The two-match suspension he picked up for verbally provoking the French captain was, in his view, "an affront, not only to me, but to the world of football". According to Marco, "In football, there have always been some things that are settled on the pitch, and players often aren't just whispering sweet nothings in each other's ears. I think that both Zidane and I were up for it."

Since then, the 6'3" Marco has become a star. Besides being a World Cup winner, he was also made a freeman of Lecce, the town of his birth. Inter, for whom he'd only made 17 first-team appearances in 2005–06, arranged its 2006–07 subscription campaign around his picture. At the age of 33, his contract with the club was extended to 2010. His mighty chest was also chosen for an advertising campaign, in which he withstood the repeated battering of a medicine ball, a 4x4 and a bulldozer without flinching ... a triumph for a true bad boy.

Things don't change. During a friendly between Sporting Portugal and Inter Milan on August 21, 2006, which ended scoreless, Materazzi pulled off another feat: he was sent off before the season had even started! ■

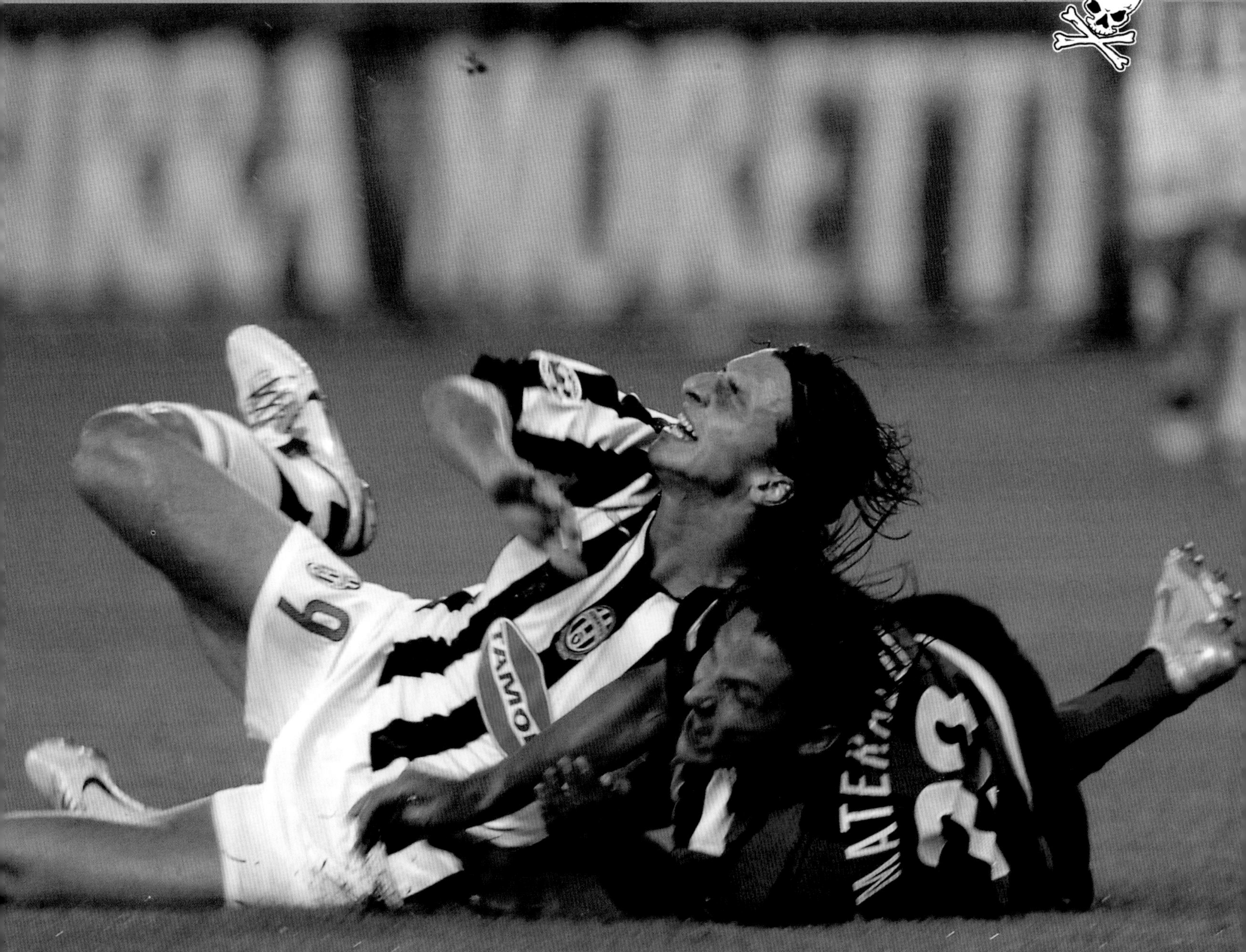

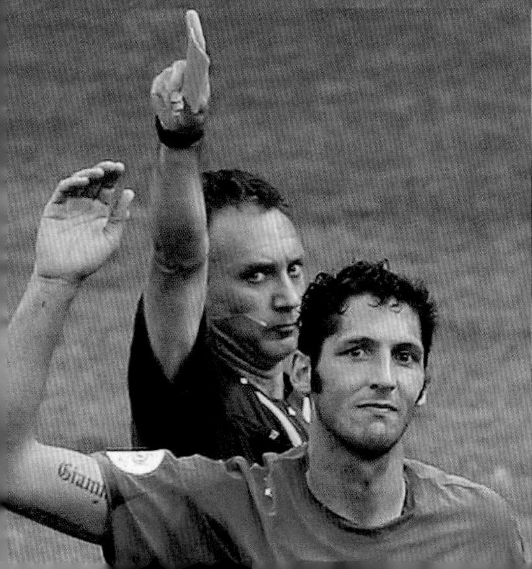

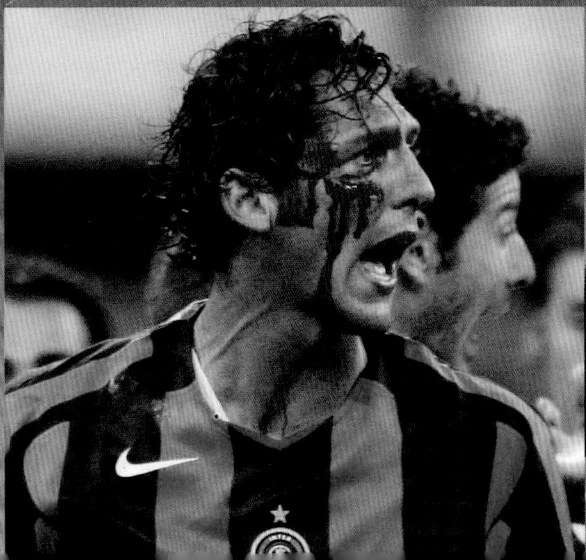

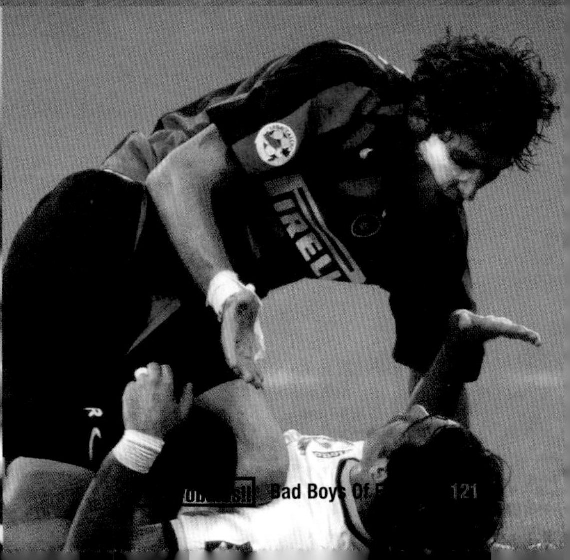

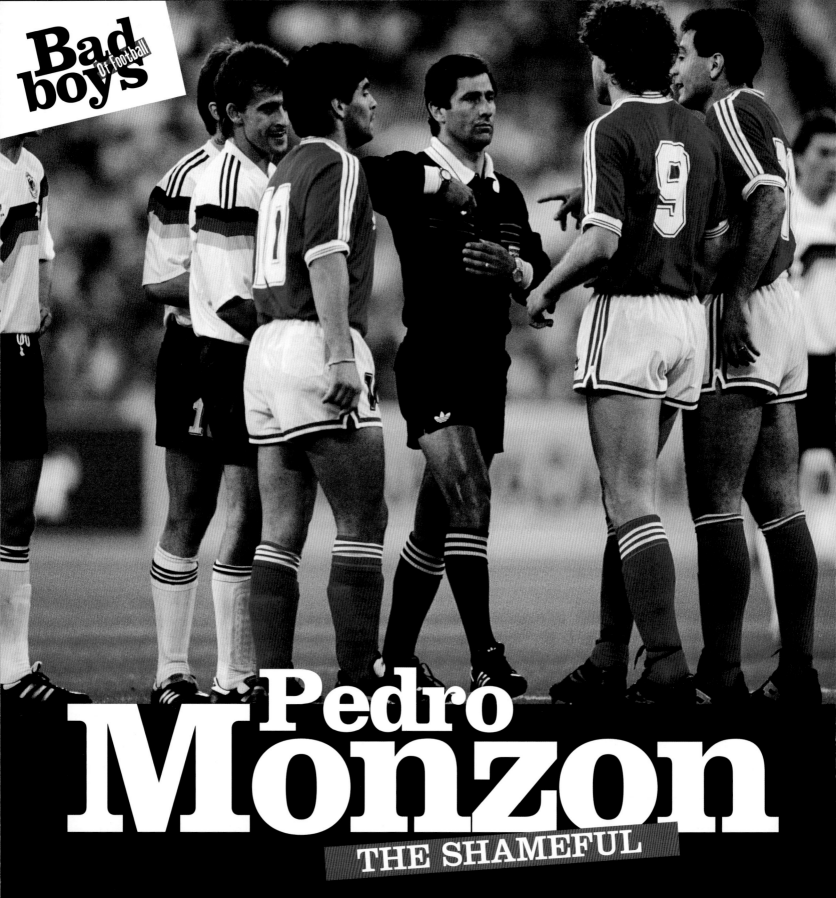

Bad boys Of Football

Pedro
Monzon

THE SHAMEFUL

the real reprobates!!

Pedro Monzon

"You can let the man or the ball past, but never both!"

You could make a case for putting Carlos Bilardo, Pedro Monzon's coach and intellectual guide, higher in the pecking order of bad boys than Monzon himself. The coach of the Argentine finalists of the 1990 World Cup undoubtedly had more tricks in his sports bag than "El Moncho", as Monzon was affectionately, if slightly condescendingly known. Monzon was essentially a loyal defender, called up to the national squad far less for his technical qualities than for his grit in tackling anywhere, any time, and never giving his direct opponent a moment's respite.

His friends described him as rough round the edges and lacking manners; even his enemies regarded him as honest and hard-working. When all's said and done, though, his countrymen liked him, because this lovable loser represented the Argentina in decline of the 1990s. At the time Argentinians were clinging on to Diego Maradona's worn studs and Bilardo's stunts, preferring to believe that the refereeing of the 1990 final between Germany and Argentina, the revenge match for 1986, went against them and that the penalty that gave victory to West Germany (1–0) was unwarranted, rather than admit that Argentina didn't really deserve to win. Pedro Monzon was the scorer of Argentina's goal in the 1–1 draw with Romania in the first round, which narrowly earned them a place in the second phase, and was therefore the player who symbolized their laborious qualification as well as the one who carried the injustice of the final defeat on his broad shoulders.

Focusing on his story alone would mean overlooking Argentina's strange 1–0 victory over Brazil in the knock-out phase. Several people, Maradona included, have since admitted that the water generously handed out by Bilardo to the Brazilians during the stoppages may well have been spiked with a sleeping pill or two … But all that is overshadowed by something that no one can take away from

Pedro Monzon: the distinction of being the first player to be sent off in a World Cup final.

Monzon came on at half-time, fired up by his coach. The Argentinians were struggling against the Germans and had only one thing in mind, to hang on for extra time and penalties. Monzon substituted Nestor Sensini and shored up a defence of sheer poetry, made up of Sergio Goycochea (keeper), Jose Serrizuela, Juan Simon and Oscar Ruggeri, the boss of the back four whose motto was: "You can let the man or the ball past, but never both!" – a motto that Monzon made his own. He had only been on the pitch for 19 minutes when a terrible tackle in the 65th minute earned him the first red card in a World Cup final (36 years after the first yellow had been brandished in any World Cup match, during the Mexico–USSR game in 1970).

History barely recalls the fact that Gustavo Dezzoti, the Argentine centre-forward, was also sent off in the 87th minute. Monzon was the only fall guy. He took the blame for all the amoral and violent Argentine players, all the second-rate bad boys, who did not even come close to their hero's level, even though he was already on the decline.

Whereas Bilardo later pursued his coaching career in Spain (notably at Seville, where his shouts of "Kill him!" to encourage his defenders were loved by television viewers), Monzon never really found a place as a coach in the South American game. Despite his four League champion titles as a player with Independiente, he failed to make his mark there. There were temporary jobs, positions with reserve teams … He tried his luck in Ecuador and Mexico at second-rate clubs, but only to suffer a further humiliation, in September 2005. While on the bench of the Ecuadorian club Olmedo, Monzon earned a two-month suspension for insulting a referee.

Monzon, who admitted having a drug and alcohol problem, proved, on this occasion, that he fully deserved his place among the bad boys. ■

"I prefer to give rather than receive."

Jose Carlos Mozer

Jose Carlos Mozer
THE FORCE OF DISSUASION

Raymond Goethals, Olympic Marseille's Belgian coach, applied simple rules to football. To build a team, start with the foundations and make sure you have solid pillars in defence to support the frame. With Jose Carlos Mozer, "Raymond the Science" would have a rock. At the heart of the Olympic defence, alongside Basile Boli, the Brazilian formed an often insurmountable wall.

A violent player? "No, I'm not violent," said Mozer at his peak in 1991. "I'm hard. Violence is attacking an opponent to try and hurt him. I use my physical force to win the ball. I make contact, without malicious intent." Come on! One could certainly say that Mozer was imposing. He based his forceful defensive game more on intimidation than dirty tricks. "I play in a position in which blows are exchanged, and I prefer to give rather than receive."

The forwards who played against him in the French league between 1989 and 1992 are best placed to say just how giving he was. They all say that from the first whistle Mozer would stop at nothing to mark his territory and keep people out. Elbows stuck out exaggeratedly, chest inflated under the white and sky-blue shirt, pelvis thrust forward in a provocative manner, his long legs tensed and ready to be wielded, Mozer had the threatening look of some great exotic bird. When he stretched out his right leg for the ball (or an opponent's foot), Olympic or Brazilian supporters hardly ever worried. No one or nothing would get past.

Basile Boli, his partner at the centre of Marseille's defence, explained in his autobiography that all that was needed to scare off the softer strikers was a bit of verbal discouragement. Just like the Berlin wall, the OM defensive rampart held strong through the force of dissuasion. As with Boli, however, there was more to Mozer's game than that. The authority with which he controlled the ball on his chest offered no hope to opponents, and his throw-ins had the same clinical precision as his tackles. Chris Waddle, another OM star at the start of the 1990s, thinks he's never seen a player as strong in the air.

At the start, like many of these avenger-style footballers, who are more often than not defenders, the kid from Bangu, in the suburbs of Rio, didn't have much going for him. Reedy and puny, he didn't have

the talent or the technical skill, and certainly not the physique, to break into the very competitive world of *carioca* football.

He was given opportunities at Botafogo and then Flamengo, but they quickly dissuaded this scrawny specimen against thinking too big or too high. It was then that the doctor of his first club in Bangu decided to play God. Jose Carlos, he decided, was missing about 15 centimetres, and he was going to help him find them, using hormonal injections. For ten months, young Mozer was injected, and nothing happened. Then, suddenly … a miracle! At the age of 16, in a very short time he shot up nearly seven inches to his full height of just over six foot.

This pact with the medicine devil came at a price. Carlos would suffer from brittle bones and frequent injuries. As for his dreams of becoming a midfield or attacking player, he could forget them. When he did finally establish himself at Flamengo it was as a central defender, and with a style all his own.

For his national team, Mozer arrived at just the right time. Brazil were desperately trying to sort out their defensive weaknesses, and coach Carlos Alberto Parreira was looking for robust players. Mozer was called up in 1983 and became one of the linchpins of a team that for three years would play un-Brazilian football, before their natural style was allowed to come through again in the 1986 World Cup in Mexico, a competition that Carlos would watch on TV, recovering from a knee operation. He would make up for it four years later by taking part in Italia 90. He was called up to the national team a total of 36 times.

The following year, during a friendly between Flamengo and FC Porto, Mozer caught the eye of the big European clubs. Porto were interested, but it was Benfica who took the prize and kept the Brazilian for two seasons. In 1989 Mozer began his adventures with Marseille, the club with which he would win three consecutive League titles and one French Cup. However, he also experienced two defeats in the finals of the European Cup, in 1988 with Benfica against PSV Eindhoven and then in 1991 with OM at Bari, against Red Star Belgrade – each time on penalties after a 0–0 draw …

Mozer returned to play at Benfica in 1993, and after finishing his playing career in the Japanese league with the Kashima Antlers, he joined the technical staff of the big Lisbon club. ∎

"Clashes, thumps and bruises are what the crowd often wants to see."

Kevin Muscat

WHY THE AGGRO?

For the French, he will always be the one who injured Christophe Dugarry in a match between Australia and France in 2001. It was a "friendly" game, played on November 11, but there would be no armistice on that day for Kevin Muscat. In the 56th minute, the Socceroos wing-back crushed the Frenchman's knee between his legs in a killer tackle from behind, resulting in a huge sprain, the start of an all-out brawl and a yellow card for the guilty party – the least he could expect.

"What made me most angry was that it wasn't in the spirit of the match. It was an awful tackle," said Dugarry after the match. "I never imagined he'd tackle me like that!" Muscat claimed that he had been wound up by Robert Pires, who had had spat in his face.

The problem with Muscat is that his career has been spattered with examples of extreme behaviour. In the Premier League, he made a firm enemy of Dennis Bergkamp and also of Ian Wright, who refused to say his name and called him "nobody". Muscat even received the honour of being named by the press as one of the biggest butchers of the Premier League. The Australian was in good company, alongside hard men such as ex-Gunners Tony Adams and Lee Dixon, former Manchester United player Roy Keane (see page 112) and the Wimbledon bad boys. In 1999 Nottingham Forest striker Ian Wright was sent off in a match against Wolverhampton Wanderers, the club Muscat joined after Crystal Palace, for landing an uppercut on the Australian, who had clearly subjected the player to special treatment throughout the match. The striker's comments were unequivocal: "It was the first time in my life that I don't regret what I did at all. I generally apologize, but he doesn't deserve it. It was my pleasure!"

Owing to his tendency to show his studs, the nickname "the most hated man in England" was pinned on Muscat, and he even ended up in court. On February 24, 2004, he was ordered by the London High Court of Justice to pay £250,000 in damages to Matty Holmes – a kind of testimonial to this wild tackler. It was end of a long story. Muscat had seriously injured the Charlton striker four years earlier in a Cup match. With a shin fracture just above the ankle, Holmes endured a long period of rehabilitation but played only one more match with his club before finally calling time on his career in 2000, at the age of just 29.

"My lawsuit was based on the income I lost on account of the injury," explained Holmes at the time. "My family suffered too. I was emotionally and physically tired of life." To convince the court, Holmes's lawyers demonstrated Muscat's often violent behaviour. They established that the Australian international had seriously injured eight other players with dangerous tackles. For the first time, British justice recognized the deliberate intent of a player and found in favour of the plaintiff. Muscat and his then club, Wolverhampton Wanderers, were even ordered to pay £500,000 in court costs.

After spells with Crystal Palace, Wolves, Glasgow Rangers and Millwall (in the Second Division), Muscat returned to play in his native Australia. In 2006, at the age of 33, he was still on the rampage in Melbourne, and regretting nothing: "FIFA is obviously now trying to clean up the game, but lots of people are asking whether this approach will improve it. If the matches attract a lot of people, it's because it's very high-level competition. Clashes, thumps and bruises are what the crowd often wants to see." It's perhaps not surprising that in Australia he continues to pick up suspensions. ∎

"I tried to hold myself back to avoid picking up so many cards."

Cyril Rool

FRENCH QUALITY

the real
reprobates!!
Cyril Rool

This French hero has explored every conceivable way of getting sent off. He is a specialist in the field, an expert, in fact a French record-holder … Looking at his angelic face, you wouldn't think twice about giving the ball to Cyril Rool. It might even be better if you did – because he'd stop at nothing to get it.

As a young player he compensated for an average build (approx. 5'7" and 11 stone) with phenomenal energy and a highly intense style of play. "I learned to play football in the tough areas of Marseille. When I was in the Cadets and the Juniors, you had to be strong when you went to some places, so you didn't get pushed around. These were proper matches, we got stuck in and sometimes there would be fights. Because I didn't go to a training school, this was where I learned my mental strength. I'm still an impulsive player and ready to retaliate. It shows with me, because I don't hide anything. And I say what's on my mind." That's Cyril Rool all over, a victim of his own honesty, a good bloke, just a bit on the direct side.

In 1993, on his Division Two debut with Bastia (where he stayed until 1998), his temperament went down a storm at the Furiani stadium. "When I started in Corsica, it was difficult because I wasn't in my element. I played the way I used to in the youth matches. I was hot-headed and used to lose it for a few seconds. I got a lot of cards at the start of my career because I couldn't let anything go. I wasn't bad, just too open."

The arrival of Frederic Antonetti helped him to cultivate his reputation as a hard man. The young Corsican coach who, when a player himself, was never averse to picking up cards, suggested that Cyril shave his head. With his new look, Rool could take on the role of bad boy. Fouls, disputed decisions and red cards all mounted up. At the end of the 2005–06 season he already had 19 red cards, making him a record-holder in France and something of an expert in the art of being sent off.

But life isn't easy for a bad boy! As well as his opponents, he had to put up with the coaches. "I had problems with quite a few of them," he confessed, "because they wouldn't tolerate me being sent off any more. I don't think I'd ever have made it anywhere other than Bastia. It's the only place where they had the patience to wait for me to calm down and supported me, like a family."

Like any self-respecting bad boy, Rool accepted the role (first at Bastia, then at Lens, Marseille, Monaco, Lens again, Bordeaux and Nice). "We need guys with character. If all players were the same, it would be boring. There are loads of dreary matches. I'm not asking for fights to spice up the matches, but at least commitment and serious duels." >

"Nowadays in France, just sneeze and you'll get a card."

Urged by his coaches, however, he did make an effort to control himself, particularly at Lens. "I tried to hold myself back to avoid picking up so many cards, but it wasn't me. My opponents found it easier to get past me. You have to follow your nature. Except when I go too far, my temperament is my strength. I put up with my reputation as a hard player. My close friends know that I'm not nuts and that I don't wind anyone up."

Rool also promised that he'd matured, that he was calmer, even though his game wasn't always within the letter of the law. According to him, it was a national problem. "Nowadays, in France just sneeze and you'll get a card. I feel a bit out of place because they don't like you even to tickle your opponent or back into him. Every time it happens, you'd think someone had been murdered. The culture in Argentina and England is the opposite, which is why their football is fun to watch. In Italy, in the derbies, they're not there to exchange gifts, they get stuck in. It's a bit like wrestling: it's not that pretty, but at least it's exciting … As for the cards, they find it easier to give one to me than to some of the others …"

For Rool the problem is one of injustice. In 2004 he was wrongly sent off during a Marseille–Bordeaux match. The disciplinary committee exonerated him, but it was yet another stain on his reputation. During the Lyon–Bordeaux match on May 15, 2005, he openly insulted the referee, Mr Garibian, who had no choice but to send him off, but it was because Florent Malouda had just fractured his nose! Who wouldn't have reacted angrily?

This is how Cyril Rool, quiet and calm in his day-to-day life, can suddenly turn into the Hulk on the pitch, the footballing Mr Hyde. But he's not there to be loved – he's clear about that: "On the street, I pass unnoticed, which is good. I'm not trying to make people like me. In fact, I don't like being talked about." ∎

"If Battiston really wants me to, I'll pay his dentist's bill […] There's no place for compassion among professionals."

Harald Schumacher
PROFESSION: BUTCHER

the real reprobates!!
H. Schumacher

In France, he's seen as a sort of evil genius, the archetypal breaker of bones and shatterer of dreams. More specifically, as the player who stopped Patrick Battiston and the French team in their tracks, in their attempt to reach a first and well-deserved World Cup final.

Anyone who saw the 1982 World Cup semi-final in Seville between France and West Germany will remember how Schumacher raced out of goal and launched himself, feet in the air, eyes and elbow aimed at the jaw of the French midfielder who had darted forward, alone, on goal. All without a glance at the ball, and afterwards no excuse, no act of contrition. No, while the crumpled body of the player he'd just collided with was being carried off on a stretcher, the guilty party, Harald Schumacher, turned his back on the scene and went on chewing his gum. Battiston was taken to Seville hospital with a fracture of the second cervical vertebra and teeth smashed to smithereens, and would spend more than two months recovering. Adding insult to injury, Schumacher's only comment after the match (won by Germany on penalties after ending in a 3–3 draw) was "If Battiston really wants me to, I'll pay his dentist's bill."

One week after the event, Schumacher went to visit Battiston, who was recuperating with his family in Metz. Was he going to apologize? No, only to explain, or rather justify his behaviour. "It's part of the risk you face and it could happen to anyone. It could well happen to me tomorrow. There's no place for compassion among professionals." Accepting that he was the victim of circumstances, and despite what Schumacher had put him through, Battiston generously consented to the visit.

Schumacher would not have got away with it in today's game. Referees are under much stricter instructions, and forwards are better protected. The game is more fluid and the actions of bad boys are much more likely to be penalized. In this situation, Schumacher would probably have picked up a red card and the match would have turned out differently – assuming that the referee had seen the goalkeeper's horrendous foul. In Seville, Charles Corver didn't even blow for a free-kick! But that was 1982. Unforgivable though it was, Schumacher's foul was committed in an era when violence on the pitch was controlled far less than it is today. The 1980s were kind to hard men. >

"I didn't want to go and apologize, because I didn't feel guilty."

But it was also a time of increasingly high stakes in football. For many managers, and players too, the common philosophy was to keep sentiment out of it: all that mattered was winning, whatever the price, even if the price was infamy. Harald Schumacher was saying the same thing the day after the final: "There's a certain theatre to the game. I admit that people think I'm a lout, but when you play should you listen only to your heart, or to reason?"

His pitiless attitude accentuated the scandal, as millions saw the image of the man on the ground, injured, and that of his aggressor, who apparently felt nothing. "I didn't want to go and apologize, because I didn't feel guilty. It's not in my nature to apologize when I don't think I've done anything wrong. When an apology is insincere, it means nothing. But I felt as if I aged five years that night. More than 20 years later, I've no regrets. I've always said it was just an accident. Even if people keep going on about it, it was a part of my life and I just deal with it," said Schumacher.

Could it be that the man the French called "the Butcher of Seville" was simply a winner through and through, an iron-willed giant in a team that was hardly a bunch of choirboys? A bloke whose priority, after bringing Battiston down, was to keep his concentration for the remainder of this decisive match?

In Germany, where they nicknamed him "Toni", his most

controversial action was to publish an autobiography in 1987 in which he raised suspicions of substance abuse by members of the 1982 national team. These accusations led to Schumacher's contract with FC Cologne being broken and his being permanently dropped from the German team.

Anyone who has had a close look at Harald Schumacher's hands will know that the keeper has not given less than 100 per cent during his 24 years in the professional game. Goalkeepers' fingers tend to have taken a hammering, but none more spectacularly than Schumacher's. Not one of the player's fingers is straight. They are all scarred and slanting, haphazardly redesigned by multiple fractures.

Schumacher may well have dished out plenty of hammerings, but he has also received his share in return, in his 15 years at Cologne, then at Fenerbahce in Turkey, and finally at Bayern. During those years, on the evening of a defeat, Toni would return home in silence and let off steam for hours on end with a punching ball. To test his willpower and resistance to pain he would also stub out cigarettes on his forearms.

After Schumacher's playing career came to an end, he moved into coaching and took charge of the specialist goalkeeping sessions at Leverkusen. In 2004 he left the club and set out to build a new reputation, as a trainer. ∎

Diego Simeone

THE HOT-BLOODED GAUCHO

Diego Simeone

"I love it when the rival fans whistle at me. I go into a trance. I've got a rugged style, I go in for contact."

Hard, irascible, combative … The Argentine Diego Simeone is undeniably a bit of all of these things – maybe more than a bit, since this midfield loudmouth and tireless winner of the ball has always known how to pull his team-mates along in his wake. This certainly explains why he was favoured by all the Argentina coaches between 1988 and 2002 (Carlos Bilardo, Alfio Basile, Daniel Passarella and Marcelo Bielsa), and played three World Cup tournaments in 1994, 1998 and 2002.

When it came to the will to win, Simeone had it in spades. He generally committed the first foul of the match, to let the opposition's No. 10 know that he was likely to be in for a bad night. It's his run-ins with the play-makers that have forged his legend. In the second round of the knock-out stage of the 1998 World Cup final against England, after cleverly winding up David Beckham for much of the match, the cunning Diego made as big a meal as possible of the Spice Boy's retaliatory flick of the leg, and Danish referee Kim Milton Nielson saw red. England went out on penalties after their 10 men had held on through extra time for a 2–2 draw.

Several months later, Simeone admitted to the BBC: "Let's just say I fell convincingly at a tense point in the match. I was clever, because I more or less forced the referee to show the red card, although there was no doubt Beckham only deserved a yellow. I think the referee was punishing the intention more than the action itself." In Argentina's

1–0 victory over Nigeria in the first round of the 2002 World Cup he produced a number of special tackles for another No. 10, Jay-Jay Okocha.

Despite the hot-blooded nature of this highly charged gaucho, however, Simeone was sent off only once in 106 games for his national team (which, at the time, was a record for an Argentinian player). Aware that his reputation was an advantage, he ceaselessly fuelled it with well-chosen statements, such as: "I love it when the rival fans whistle at me. I go into a trance. I've got a rugged style, I go in for contact. A team needs players like me, so that the stars can shine."

When he arrived in Rome and first put on the Lazio shirt, Simeone greeted the club's "Ultras" by holding his crotch, doubtless to reassure them that he was as combative as ever. Yet it would be wrong to think of him just as a water-carrier and a purveyor of over-the-top tackles. The Argentine also had a very sound technique and a powerful style in the air. His successes with his clubs (the Cup and League double with both Atletico Madrid in 1996 and Lazio in 2002, and the UEFA Cup with Inter Milan in 1998) and with the national team (the Copa America in 1991 and 1993) bear testament to this. "People forget that I've scored more than 100 goals over my career, eleven of these for the national team," he stresses, "so I'm not that limited."

After retiring from the pitch in February 2006, Diego Simeone began a coaching career at Racing Club in Buenos Aires. ■

"Only efficiency counts for me, there's no room for aesthetics."

Patrick **Vieira**

THE OCTOPUS

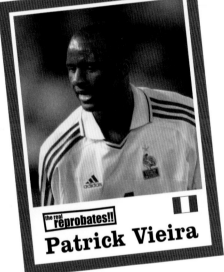

Patrick Vieira

Ah, good old Paddy! With his round face and gentle eyes, you would give him the captain's armband (as they did at Arsenal, as they do in the French team) without a moment's hesitation. However, Patrick Vieira's relationships with opponents and referees alike have been consistently fraught, and strewn with red and yellow cards. As it happens, it was also a red, given to Marcel Desailly, that gave Vieira the opportunity to come on to the pitch in the 1998 World Cup final and then pass to Emmanuel Petit, his Arsenal team-mate, for the third French goal in their 3–0 win against Brazil.

The tall young Vieira (he's almost 6'3") owed his place in the French team to his long, thin and untiring legs, which would earn him the nickname "the Octopus" in England, to his lungs, which he believes he helps by inelegantly daubing decongestant to the neck of his shirt, and to his willingness get stuck into the dirty work when on the pitch. "Only efficiency counts for me, there's no room for aesthetics. It's what the position needs. I've got to get out there and do what needs to be done, make sure players respect me. I've always been told that the more scared you are of going in for contact, the worse you'll do, so I go in for contact. A player who's a coward will never do well at this level."

His professional debut in France with Cannes, from 1993 to 1995, was impressive enough to earn him a transfer to AC Milan. But he was still a bit soft: in 49 matches in the French Division One he had only picked up 16 yellow cards and a single red. Whatever the reason, he didn't play at the San Siro. One year later, he was welcomed to London by Arsene Wenger, who had just arrived at Arsenal. It was with the Gunners that "the Long One" (the nickname he would receive two years later from new team-mate Thierry Henry) carved out his reputation and a place in midfield, sometimes thanks to his elbows, which he often liked to spread on returning to earth after leaping to head the ball. >

"I've never been sent off after wanting to hurt an opponent."

One of the common traits of the great champions is their ability to step up a gear from the start of a match. This is true of Vieira, an angel off the pitch but an insatiable hard man when a match starts. "I'm fundamentally a nice guy," confessed Pat. "I don't lose my temper when I'm not playing football. But when you're too nice, you're taken for an idiot!"

On January 17, 1998, he was sent off for hotly disputing a penalty. He failed to learn his lesson, because a month later he was sent off again following a second yellow card for violent tackling. Then, in December of the same year, he picked up a red card and a three-match

suspension for dangerous use of his elbow. Vieira was unapologetic: "I'm an expansive guy on the pitch. I'll never change my style of play because it's my number-one quality. Let's put my reaction down to naivety. There's no smoke without fire." In other words, it's just that people provoke him and he reacts. It's a familiar story with bad boys, who would undoubtedly never have any problems with referees if they weren't constantly being sought out on all corners of the pitch for no reason.

Ten months later, however, Vieira finally had to admit that he was at fault. On October 3, 1999 he drew universal condemnation by spitting on West Ham's Neil Ruddock. The FA suspended him for six matches and hit him with a £45,000 fine – the largest fine ever given to a player. "I portrayed a bad image of myself," admitted the Frenchman. "It was low. I was ashamed when I saw it on TV and in the papers."

In the year 2000 Vieira reached new heights. After winning the European Championship with the French team, he started the season with a bang – two sendings-off within 48 hours, on August 19 and 21, following an elbow and two successive warnings in less than five minutes. The Highbury crowd idolized him even more. Vieira allowed himself to theorize: "There's a certain amount of jealousy in all places of work. Jealousy is part of life. I only ever reacted, I never struck first."

In September 2002, he courted further controversy after receiving his eighth red card since his arrival in England. The press called him violent. He half-heartedly defended himself: "I've never been sent off after wanting to hurt an opponent." On February 1, 2005, against Manchester United, he had another clash with Gary Neville who, according to United manager Alex Ferguson, was "physically provoked by Patrick Vieira in the corridor". The match ended 4–2 in United's favour, consolidating their success, in the previous match, of ending Arsenal's 49-match unbeaten run in the League. The London player's explanation: "I wasn't trying to wind Neville up, just sort a few things out with him."

Nevertheless, "the Octopus" bared his teeth again in November 2005 when his autobiography was published in England. He used it to fling mud at his enemies, notably Manchester United's exasperating Dutch striker Ruud Van Nistelrooy, calling him "cowardly", "deceitful" and a "cheat".

In the eyes of the English fans, the biggest foul ever committed by the player who succeeded the emblematic Tony Adams as captain

of Arsenal was when, in the summer of 2005, he quit the club to join Juventus. When the two clubs met in the Champions League in March 2006, the press went mad, and when Arsenal beat Juventus 2–0 in the first leg at Highbury, one headline read: "Who needs Vieira?" After a killer tackle on Arsenal player Jose Antonio Reyes, Paddy received a yellow card, meaning he would be suspended for the second leg (he'd already received a card in the previous round). Highbury chanted: "Vieira, who are you?" His Italian season, blighted by a groin strain, finished badly. After the scandal surrounding the referees chosen by Lucciano Moggi, the Turin club's sporting director, Juve were stripped of their League championship and were relegated to Serie B.

Vieira threw himself back into it again with the French team in the 2006 World Cup. (He had also suffered the insult of being sent off playing for France, for allegedly diving no less, in September 2004 during a 2–0 win against the Faro Islands.) He sounded his team's reveille by not only being France's best player in most of the matches, but also he scored the first goal in their 2–0 victory over Togo on his thirtieth birthday. Defeat in this game would have resulted in elimination for France. In terms of discipline, he left it to Zidane to pick up the bulk of the cards. Vieira was cautioned only once.

After transferring to Inter, Vieira came face to face in training with Marco Materazzi (see page 118), who scored Italy's goal and got Zidane sent off in the World Cup final, without any apparent animosity. But if you spend too much time with bad boys … With his new club, he began by being sent off in the Champions League after picking up two yellow cards in the match against Sporting Portugal. One week later, during a League match against AS Rome, he verbally abused the referee who had dared to send him off after a further two cautions. Vieira obviously remembered a lot from his Italian lessons the first time round in 1996.

The Italian League's disciplinary committee also recognized his flair for foreign languages: "The clear content of the phrase uttered left no doubt as to who the insult was directed at, as to the fact that he was fully aware of what he said and as to the meaning of the words used." He was suspended for three matches. Three more matches. ∎

Index

PHOTOGRAPHIC CREDITS

L'Equipe: pp. 12–13, 16, 18, 21, 35, 65, 102, 103, 107, 124, 132, 134; *Alain de Martignac/ L'Equipe:* pp. 54, 99, 101, 128; *Alain Landrain/L'Equipe:* p. 71; *Bernard Matussiere/L'Equipe:* p. 105; *Bernard Papon/L'Equipe:* p. 45; *Bruno Fablet/L'Equipe:* p. 78; *Daniel Bardou/ L'Equipe:* p. 98; *Didier Fevre/L'Equipe:* p. 91; *Franck Nataf/L'Equipe:* p. 99; *Jacky Delorme/ L'Equipe:* p. 96; *Jean-Claude Pichon/L'Equipe:* pp. 36, 52, 100; *Pierre Lablatiniere/L'Equipe:* pp. 63, 123; *Pierre Lahalle/L'Equipe:* pp. 50, 51, 120; *Richard Martin/L'Equipe:* p. 86; *Marc Francotte/L'Equipe:* p. 62; *Nicolas Luttiau/L'Equipe:* pp. 48, 139; *OFFSIDE/ Presse Sports:* pp. 34, 36, 74, 75, 77, 84, 85, 112, 140, 141; *Miguelez/Presse Sports:* p. 61; *Grazia Neri/Presse Sports:* pp. 69, 120; *PICS United/Presse Sports:* pp. 43, 72, 86, 114, 117, 127; *PIKO/Presse Sports:* p. 35; *Popperfoto/Presse Sports:* pp. 19, 20, 24, 37, 46, 60, 82, 83; *Richiardi/Presse Sports:* pp. 51, 52, 53; *Witters/Presse Sports:* pp. 12–13, 53, 133, 139.

Abaca/Empics: pp. 22–3, 28, 32, 33, 44, 80, 93, 109, 115, 137. *AFP:* pp. 23, 27, 30, 35, 39, 64, 67, 70, 73, 76, 87, 89, 91, 113, 126, 129, 130, 137. *DPPI:* pp. 13, 15, 26, 29, 42, 58, 79, 81, 90, 106, 111, 115, 131, 134. *Icon Sport:* pp. 15, 40, 66, 68, 116. *Panoramic:* pp. 4-5, 14, 25, 31, 92, 104, 110, 119, 134. *Reuters/ MAXPPP:* pp. 6, 17, 41, 47, 49, 55, 118, 121. *SIPA:* pp. 59, 108.

AUTHOR'S ACKNOWLEDGEMENTS

Not being a bad boy himself, the author wishes to thank the following people for their help and advice: Marc Beauge • Baptiste Blanchet • Jean-Michel Brochen • Daniele Coussot • Thierry Dengerma • and the L'Equipe documentation service • Pierre-Marie Descamps • Gerard Ejnes • Gerard Ernault • Laurence Gauthier • Jacques Hennaux • Yann Hildwein • Vincent Laudet • Gilles Montgermont • Christian Naitslimane • Matthieu Neel • Gerard Schallr • Pierre Serisier • Francois Thomazeau • Alexandre Valente. Without them, and especially without Olivier Hellard, who initiated the project, the bad boys of football would never have been able to be celebrated in this book.